Best of Country
Appetizers

Start the Party with Crowd-Pleasing Appetizers!

EVERY GOOD PARTY begins with great-tasting appetizers, be it a casual gathering of family and friends or a more formal affair. Whatever the occasion, the 264 festive finger foods and beverages in this *Best of Country Appetizers* cookbook will make your celebration a success!

This brand-new recipe collection is brimming with plate-filling ideas from past issues of *Taste of Home* magazine and its "sister" publications.

Fellow cooks from across the country shared the crowd-pleasing recipes, which have proven popular at all sorts of parties and other special occasions. Our Test Kitchen staff prepared and taste-tested each dish as well, selecting it for a book we're proud to call "The Best".

You'll impress your guests when you set out any of the appealing hot and cold appetizers, creamy spreads and dips, savory snack mixes and nuts, and thirst-quenching beverages found inside...in fact, folks will eagerly stand in line for the tasty tidbits!

Helpful tips we've sprinkled throughout the cookbook will serve as a guide when preparing these hors d'oeuvres. You'll learn how many appetizers to plan per person, serving suggestions and so much more. We've also included full-color photos of many recipes, so you can see what they look like before you start cooking.

Invite *Best of Country Appetizers* into your cookbook collection, and its bite-sized morsels and beverages will be the talk of your parties!

Editor: Jean Steiner
Art Director: Kathy Crawford
Food Editor: Janaan Cunningham
Associate Food Editors: Coleen Martin, Diane Werner
Senior Recipe Editor: Sue A. Jurack
Recipe Editor: Janet Briggs
Associate Editors: Beth Wittlinger, Heidi Reuter Lloyd
Food Photography: Rob Hagen, Dan Roberts
Senior Food Photography Artist: Stephanie Marchese
Food Photography Artist: Julie Ferron
Photo Studio Manager: Anne Schimmel
Chairman and Founder: Roy Reiman

©2004 Reiman Media Group, Inc.
5400 S. 60th St., Greendale WI 53129
International Standard Book Number: 0-89821-409-2
Library of Congress Control Number: 2004092616
All rights reserved.
Printed in U.S.A.

Pictured on Front Cover: Feta Bruschetta (p. 63), Cheddar Fondue (p. 24), Sugar 'n' Spice Nuts (p. 92) and Lemon-Berry Pitcher Punch (p. 103).

Best of Country
Appetizers

Makes a Great Gift!

To order additional copies of the *Best of Country Appetizers* book, specify item number 33699 and send $15.99 (plus $3.95 shipping/insured delivery for one book, $4.50 for two or more) to: Country Store, Suite 6806, P.O. Box 990, Greendale WI 53129-0990. To order by credit card, call toll-free 1-800/558-1013 or visit our Web site at *www.reimanpub.com*.

CREAMY GUACAMOLE

CREAMY CARAMEL DIP

CREAMY THYME SPREAD

TURKEY TACO DIP

HERBED GARLIC CHEESE SPREAD

FESTIVE PUMPKIN DIP

DIPS & SPREADS

mCreamy Guacamole

(Pictured above)

Phyllis Allan, Vero Beach, Florida

As a transplanted New Englander, I was anxious to use some of Florida's fresh fruits in new recipes. I came across this one and it quickly became a favorite.

- 1 medium ripe avocado, halved, seeded and peeled
- 2 teaspoons lime juice
- 2 packages (3 ounces *each*) cream cheese, softened
- 1/2 teaspoon Worcestershire sauce
- 1/4 teaspoon salt
- 1/4 teaspoon hot pepper sauce
Tortilla chips

In a small mixing bowl, beat avocado with lime juice. Add the cream cheese, Worcestershire sauce, salt and hot pepper sauce; beat until smooth. Serve with tortilla chips. Refrigerate leftovers. **Yield:** 1-1/3 cups.

Pecan-Date Cheese Ball

(Pictured at right)

Sue Broyles, Cherokee, Texas

This lightly sweet cheese ball is great to have on hand when we crave something creamy or if company drops by. It's even nice enough for the holidays.

- 1 teaspoon ground mustard
- 1 teaspoon water
- 2 packages (8 ounces *each*) cream cheese, softened

- 1/4 cup mayonnaise
- 1/4 teaspoon ground nutmeg
- 2 cups (8 ounces) shredded cheddar cheese
- 1 cup chopped dates
- 1 cup chopped pecans
Crackers

In a small bowl, dissolve the mustard in water; let stand for 10 minutes. In a mixing bowl, beat cream cheese and mayonnaise until smooth. Add nutmeg and mustard mixture. Stir in cheese and dates. Chill for 15 minutes. Shape into a ball; roll in pecans. Chill. Serve with crackers. Refrigerate leftovers. **Yield:** 3-1/2 cups (4-inch ball).

Blue Cheese Garlic Dip

Ron Treadaway, Acworth, Georgia

I like to serve chicken wings with this creamy dip. If you like, you can substitute crab for the shrimp.

- 1 jar (12 ounces) refrigerated blue cheese dressing
- 1 can (4-1/2 ounces) tiny shrimp, rinsed and chopped
- 4 green onions, thinly sliced
- 1 to 2 garlic cloves, minced
- 1/4 teaspoon celery seed
- 1/4 teaspoon dried thyme
- 1/8 to 1/4 teaspoon cayenne pepper
- 1/8 to 1/4 teaspoon ground mustard
- 1/8 to 1/4 teaspoon white pepper
- 1/8 to 1/4 teaspoon hot pepper sauce
Fresh vegetables *or* crackers

In a bowl, combine the first 10 ingredients; mix well. Cover and chill for at least 2 hours. Serve with vegetables or crackers. Refrigerate leftovers. **Yield:** about 2 cups.

Roasted Vegetables with Dip

(Pictured above)

Melinda Sheridan, Pittsburg, Kansas

These colorful vegetables and zippy dip taste so good it never occurs to my family that they're eating something nutritious and low in fat.

✓ Uses less fat, sugar or salt. Includes Nutritional Analysis and Diabetic Exchanges.

1/2 cup fat-free mayonnaise
1/4 cup fat-free sour cream
2 tablespoons salsa
1 garlic clove, minced
12 fresh mushrooms
1 medium sweet red pepper, cut into 1-1/2-inch pieces
1 medium green pepper, cut into 1-1/2-inch pieces
1 medium red onion, cut into wedges
1 medium yellow summer squash, cut into 1-1/2-inch pieces
1 tablespoon olive oil

For dip, combine the first four ingredients in a small bowl; refrigerate for 30 minutes or overnight. Toss vegetables with oil. Place in a single layer in an ungreased 15-in. x 10-in. x 1-in. baking pan. Bake, uncovered, at 450° for 10 minutes or until crisp-tender. Serve with the dip. Refrigerate leftovers. **Yield:** 8 servings (1 cup dip).

Nutritional Analysis: 1 cup of vegetables with 2 tablespoons of dip equals 65 calories, 140 mg sodium, 1 mg cholesterol, 10 g carbohydrate, 2 g protein, 2 g fat. **Diabetic Exchange:** 2 vegetable.

Creamy Sourdough Snack

Darelyn Payes, Hayward, California

I received many compliments on this rich dip when I served it at my mom's 50th birthday party.

1-1/2 cups (12 ounces) sour cream
2 packages (3 ounces *each*) cream cheese
1/2 cup chopped green onions
1 teaspoon Worcestershire sauce
2 cups (8 ounces) shredded sharp cheddar cheese
1-1/2 cups cubed fully cooked ham
1 round loaf (1 pound) sourdough bread
Chopped fresh parsley, optional

In a saucepan, combine sour cream, cream cheese, onions and Worcestershire sauce; cook and stir over low heat until blended. Add cheese and ham; cook and stir until cheese is melted and ham is heated through.

Cut off top of loaf; carefully hollow out top and bottom, leaving a 1/2-in. shell. Cut bread into cubes. Pour dip into shell; sprinkle with parsley if desired. Serve with bread cubes. Refrigerate leftovers. **Yield:** 3-1/2 cups.

Clever Containers

Place dips in colorful edible bowls such as red or green cabbage shells, or cored sweet red, yellow or green peppers. Fruit dips can be spooned into melon, orange or grapefruit shells.

1/8 teaspoon pepper
1 tablespoon all-purpose flour
1 tablespoon cold water
Red food coloring, optional
Pretzels

In a saucepan, combine the first seven ingredients; whisk over medium heat until smooth. Combine flour and cold water until smooth; add to cranberry mixture. Bring to a boil; cook and stir for 2 minutes. Transfer to a bowl; stir in food coloring if desired. Cover and chill overnight. Serve with pretzels. **Yield:** 2 cups.

Creamy Caramel Dip

(Pictured below)

Karen Laubman, Spruce Grove, Alberta

Because I feed three hungry "men" (my husband, a member of the Royal Canadian Mounted Police, and our two little boys), I love satisfying snacks that are easy to make like this dip. I modified a friend's recipe. We sure appreciate this cool light treat in the summertime.

1 package (8 ounces) cream cheese, softened
3/4 cup packed brown sugar
1 cup (8 ounces) sour cream
2 teaspoons vanilla extract
2 teaspoons lemon juice
1 cup cold milk
1 package (3.4 ounces) instant vanilla pudding mix
Assorted fresh fruit

In a mixing bowl, beat cream cheese and brown sugar until smooth. Add the sour cream, vanilla, lemon juice, milk and pudding mix, beating well after each addition. Cover and chill for at least 1 hour. Serve as a dip for fruit. Refrigerate leftovers. **Yield:** 3-1/2 cups.

Ruby-Red Pretzel Dip

(Pictured above)

Grace Yaskovic, Branchville, New Jersey

Plain pretzels get a pretty coating and tangy taste from this thick, festive blend.

1 can (16 ounces) jellied cranberry sauce
3/4 cup sugar
1/4 cup vinegar
1 teaspoon ground ginger
1 teaspoon ground mustard
1/4 teaspoon ground cinnamon

Calico Cheese Dip

(Pictured above)

Ellen Keck, Granger, Indiana

As soon as my husband tasted this tantalizing dip at a party, he suggested I get the recipe...not knowing I'd already asked the hostess for it! Attractive and zesty, it's one of my most popular appetizers.

- 4 cups (16 ounces) shredded Monterey Jack cheese
- 1 can (4 ounces) chopped green chilies
- 1 can (2-1/4 ounces) sliced ripe olives, drained
- 4 green onions, sliced
- 3 medium tomatoes, seeded and diced
- 1/2 cup minced fresh parsley
- 1 envelope Italian salad dressing mix

Tortilla chips

In a mixing bowl, combine the cheese, chilies, olives, onions, tomatoes and parsley. Prepare salad dressing mix according to package directions; pour over cheese mixture and mix well. Serve immediately with tortilla chips. Refrigerate leftovers. **Yield:** 6 cups.

Linda's BLT Spread

(Pictured at right)

Linda Nilsen, Anoka, Minnesota

This spread is a different way to enjoy the winning combination of bacon, lettuce and tomato. It's especially flavorful using fresh garden tomatoes!

- 1/2 cup sour cream
- 1/2 cup mayonnaise
- 1/2 pound bacon, cooked and crumbled
- 1 small tomato, diced

Small lettuce leaves

Toasted snack bread *or* crackers

Fresh vegetables

In a bowl, combine sour cream, mayonnaise and bacon; mix well. Stir in tomato. Serve with lettuce on bread or crackers, or use as a dip for vegetables. Refrigerate leftovers. **Yield:** 1-1/2 cups.

Crab Cheese Fondue

Mary Houchin, Swansea, Illinois

We used to host fondue parties regularly with our friends and tried to outdo each other with the most wonderful recipes. This cheesy blend with its crab flavor was always a hit.

- 3/4 cup milk
- 1/2 cup condensed cream of mushroom *or* celery soup, undiluted
- 2 cups (8 ounces) shredded cheddar cheese
- 8 ounces process cheese (Velveeta), cubed
- 1 can (6 ounces) crabmeat, drained, flaked and cartilage removed
- 2 teaspoons lemon juice
- 1 garlic clove, halved

Cubed French bread, cherry tomatoes, baby zucchini, cooked new potatoes *and/or* artichoke hearts for dipping

In a saucepan, combine milk and soup until blended. Add cheeses; cook and stir over low heat until melted. Stir in crab and lemon juice; remove from the heat.

Rub the interior of a fondue pot with the cut side of garlic; discard garlic. Pour cheese mixture into pot; keep at a gentle simmer over low heat. Serve with bread cubes, tomatoes, zucchini, potatoes and/or artichoke hearts. Refrigerate leftovers. **Yield:** 3 cups.

Walnut Chicken Spread

(Pictured at right)

Joan Whelan, Green Valley, Arizona

It's a breeze to stir together this tasty chicken spread. We enjoy the mild combination of chicken, crunchy walnuts, onion and celery. It's perfect with crackers or as a sandwich filling.

  1-3/4 cups finely chopped cooked chicken
      1 cup finely chopped walnuts
    2/3 cup mayonnaise
      1 celery rib, finely chopped
      1 small onion, finely chopped
      1 teaspoon salt
    1/2 teaspoon garlic powder
Assorted crackers

In a bowl, combine the chicken, walnuts, mayonnaise, celery, onion, salt and garlic powder. Serve with crackers. Refrigerate leftovers. **Yield:** 2-1/2 cups.

Festive Appetizer Spread

(Pictured below)

Edith Howe, Woburn, Massachusetts

Our state is known for its cranberries, and there are many bogs in our area. I won first place with this recipe in a contest sponsored by our local newspaper.

      1 cup water
      1 cup sugar
      1 package (12 ounces) fresh *or* frozen cranberries
    1/2 cup apricot preserves
      2 tablespoons lemon juice
    1/3 cup slivered almonds, toasted
      1 package (8 ounces) cream cheese
Assorted crackers

In a saucepan over medium heat, bring water and sugar to a boil without stirring; boil for 5 minutes. Add cranberries; cook until berries pop and sauce is thickened, about 10 minutes. Remove from the heat.

Cut apricots in the preserves into small pieces; add to cranberry mixture. Stir in lemon juice. Cool. Add almonds. Spoon over cream cheese; serve with crackers. Refrigerate leftovers. **Yield:** about 3 cups.

Party Bean Dip

Darnele West, Lancaster, South Carolina

This colorful crowd-pleasing dip is full of flavor. A cousin made it for a family get-together a number of years ago, and we finished off every bite!

      6 bacon strips
      2 garlic cloves, minced
      1 can (15 ounces) black beans, drained, rinsed
        and mashed
  1-1/2 cups (6 ounces) shredded cheddar *or* Monterey
        Jack cheese
    2/3 cup picante sauce
    1/3 cup sliced green onions
      1 teaspoon ground cumin
Chopped sweet red and yellow peppers, optional
Minced fresh cilantro, optional
Fresh vegetables *or* tortilla chips

In a skillet over medium heat, cook bacon until crisp. Drain, reserving 1 tablespoon drippings. Crumble bacon and set aside. In the drippings, saute garlic for 1-2 minutes. Stir in beans, cheese, picante sauce, onions and cumin; mix well.

Cook over low heat until cheese is melted, stirring occasionally. Stir in bacon. Transfer to a serving bowl. Garnish with peppers and cilantro if desired. Serve with vegetables or chips. Refrigerate leftovers. **Yield:** 2-1/2 cups.

Hot Pizza Dip

(Pictured at right)

Karen Riordan, Fern Creek, Kentucky

I love this recipe because it's easy to prepare in advance and keep refrigerated. Put it in the oven when guests arrive, and by the time you've poured beverages, the dip is ready.

- 1 package (8 ounces) cream cheese, softened
- 1 teaspoon Italian seasoning
- 1/4 teaspoon garlic powder
- 2 cups (8 ounces) shredded mozzarella cheese
- 1 cup (4 ounces) shredded cheddar cheese
- 1/2 cup pizza sauce
- 1/2 cup finely chopped green pepper
- 1/2 cup finely chopped sweet red pepper

Tortilla chips *or* breadsticks

In a bowl, combine cream cheese, Italian seasoning and garlic powder; spread on the bottom of a greased 9-in. pie plate. Combine cheeses; sprinkle half over the cream cheese layer. Top with the pizza sauce and peppers. Sprinkle with the remaining cheeses. Bake at 350° for 20 minutes. Serve warm with tortilla chips or breadsticks. Refrigerate leftovers. **Yield:** about 3-1/2 cups.

Roasted Corn Salsa

(Pictured below)

Nancy Horsburgh, Everett, Ontario

This colorful salsa is worth the extra time it takes to grill the ears of corn. The flavor goes well with barbecued meats, but it's also tasty served with chips.

> ✓ Uses less fat, sugar or salt. Includes Nutritional Analysis and Diabetic Exchanges.

- 2 medium ears sweet corn in husks
- 2 medium tomatoes, chopped
- 1 small onion, chopped
- 2 tablespoons minced fresh cilantro
- 1 tablespoon lime juice
- 1 tablespoon finely chopped green pepper
- 1 tablespoon finely chopped sweet red pepper
- 1 teaspoon minced seeded jalapeno pepper
- 1/4 teaspoon salt

Dash pepper

Tortilla chips

Peel back husks of corn but don't remove; remove silk. Replace husks and tie with kitchen string. Place corn in a bowl and cover with water; soak for 20 minutes. Drain. Grill corn, covered, over medium-high heat for 20-25 minutes or until husks are blackened and corn is tender, turning several times. Cool.

Remove corn from cobs and place in a bowl. Add tomatoes, onion, cilantro, lime juice, peppers, salt and pepper. Serve with tortilla chips. **Yield:** about 2-1/2 cups.

Nutritional Analysis: One serving (1/4 cup salsa) equals 24 calories, 0 fat (0 saturated fat), 0 cholesterol, 64 mg sodium, 5 g carbohydrate, 1 g fiber, 1 g protein. **Diabetic Exchange:** 1 vegetable.

Championship Bean Dip

Wendi Wavrin Law, Omaha, Nebraska

My friends and neighbors expect me to bring this irresistible dip to every gathering. When I arrive, they ask, "You brought your bean dip, didn't you?" If there are any leftovers, we use them to make bean and cheese burritos the next day.

- 1 can (16 ounces) refried beans
- 1 cup picante sauce
- 1 cup (4 ounces) shredded Monterey Jack cheese
- 1 cup (4 ounces) shredded cheddar cheese
- 3/4 cup sour cream
- 1 package (3 ounces) cream cheese, softened
- 1 tablespoon chili powder
- 1/4 teaspoon ground cumin

Tortilla chips and salsa

In a bowl, combine first eight ingredients; transfer to a slow cooker. Cover and cook on high for 2 hours or until heated through, stirring once or twice. Serve with tortilla chips and salsa. Refrigerate leftovers. **Yield:** 4-1/2 cups.

Garden Vegetable Spread

(Pictured above)

Jan Woodall, Cadiz, Kentucky

For a tempting dip or spread, try this fresh-tasting version. It's chock-full of crunchy garden vegetables.

> ✓ Uses less fat, sugar or salt. Includes Nutritional Analysis and Diabetic Exchanges.

- 1 carton (8 ounces) fat-free spreadable cream cheese
- 1/2 cup finely chopped green pepper
- 2 celery ribs, finely chopped
- 2 medium carrots, finely chopped
- 6 radishes, finely chopped
- 4 teaspoons finely chopped onion
- 1 teaspoon dill weed
- Snack toast *and/or* pita bread

In a bowl, combine the first seven ingredients. Serve on snack toast and/or pita bread. Refrigerate leftovers. **Yield:** 3 cups.

Nutritional Analysis: One serving (2 tablespoons of spread) equals 14 calories, trace fat (trace saturated fat), 1 mg cholesterol, 59 mg sodium, 2 g carbohydrate, trace fiber, 2 g protein. **Diabetic Exchange:** Free food.

Festive Ham 'n' Cheese Spread

Cara Flora, Olathe, Colorado

My family goes wild over this mild-tasting, hearty cheese spread on all sorts of crackers.

- 2 packages (8 ounces *each*) cream cheese, softened

- 1/2 cup sour cream
- 2 tablespoons dry onion soup mix
- 1 cup chopped fully cooked ham
- 1 cup (4 ounces) shredded Swiss *or* cheddar cheese
- 1/4 cup chopped fresh parsley

In a mixing bowl, beat cream cheese, sour cream and soup mix until smooth. Stir in ham and cheese. Form into a ball or spoon into a plastic wrap-lined mold. Roll in parsley or sprinkle parsley on top. Refrigerate. **Yield:** 12-14 servings (about 4 cups).

Layered Shrimp Dip

(Pictured below)

Sue Broyles, Cherokee, Texas

People's eyes light up when I set this special snack on the table. It has a terrific combination of flavors and looks so pretty. Once folks start dipping, they can't seem to stop.

- 1 package (3 ounces) cream cheese, softened
- 6 tablespoons salsa, *divided*
- 1/2 cup cocktail sauce
- 3 cans (6 ounces *each*) small shrimp, rinsed and drained
- 1 can (2-1/4 ounces) sliced ripe olives, drained
- 1 cup (4 ounces) shredded cheddar cheese
- 1 cup (4 ounces) shredded Monterey Jack cheese
- Sliced green onions
- Tortilla chips

Combine cream cheese and 3 tablespoons salsa; spread into an ungreased 9-in. pie plate. Combine cocktail sauce and remaining salsa; spread over cream cheese. Place shrimp evenly over top. Sprinkle with olives. Combine cheeses; sprinkle over olives. Top with onions. Chill. Serve with tortilla chips. Refrigerate leftovers. **Yield:** 12-16 servings.

Blue Cheese Walnut Cheesecake

(Pictured above)
Rita Reifenstein, Evans City, Pennsylvania

This elegant party spread is smooth and creamy and has a mild blue cheese flavor. It's popular every time I serve it. Garnished with chopped walnuts, it looks like you fussed.

>   2 packages (8 ounces *each*) cream cheese, softened
>   8 ounces crumbled blue cheese
> 2-1/4 cups sour cream, *divided*
>   3 eggs
>   1/8 teaspoon pepper
>   1/2 cup chopped walnuts, toasted
> Red grapes, sliced star fruit and fresh herbs, optional
> Assorted crackers

In a mixing bowl, beat cream cheese and blue cheese until fluffy. Add 1 cup of sour cream until blended. Add eggs; beat on low speed just until combined. Stir in pepper. Pour into a greased 9-in. springform pan. Place pan on a baking sheet. Bake at 325° for 25-30 minutes or until center is almost set (top may crack). Let stand on a wire rack for 5 minutes; spread with remaining sour cream. Bake 5 minutes longer.

Cool on a wire rack for 10 minutes. Carefully run a knife around edge of pan to loosen; cool 1 hour longer. Refrigerate overnight. Remove sides of pan. Sprinkle with walnuts. Garnish with grapes, star fruit and herbs if desired. Serve with crackers. Refrigerate leftovers. **Yield:** 26 servings.

Onion Cheese Ball

Shelby Finger, Hickory, North Carolina

My husband and I and our friends from church love to dig into this creamy, savory cheese ball. It's an appealing addition to any snack buffet. Folks never guess it's as good for you as it is good-tasting.

> ✓ Uses less fat, sugar or salt. Includes Nutritional Analysis and Diabetic Exchanges.

>   1 package (8 ounces) fat-free cream cheese, softened
>   8 slices (3/4 ounce *each*) fat-free sharp cheddar cheese, cut into thin strips
>   1 small onion, diced
>   1 tablespoon Worcestershire sauce
>   1 teaspoon garlic powder
> Dash hot pepper sauce
>   1/2 cup minced fully cooked low-fat ham
> Fresh vegetables *or* reduced-fat crackers

In a mixing bowl, beat cream cheese and cheddar cheese. Add onion, Worcestershire sauce, garlic powder and hot pepper sauce; mix well. Shape into a ball and roll in ham.

Cover and refrigerate for at least 1 hour. Serve with vegetables or crackers. Refrigerate leftovers. **Yield:** 1-1/2 cups.

Nutritional Analysis: One 2-tablespoon serving (calculated without crackers or vegetables) equals 24 calories, 198 mg sodium, 2 mg cholesterol, 2 g carbohydrate, 4 g protein, trace fat. **Diabetic Exchange:** 1/2 lean meat.

3/4 cup fat-free milk
1/2 cup (4 ounces) fat-free sour cream
1 package (3.4 ounces) instant coconut cream
   pudding mix
Fresh pineapple, grapes and strawberries *or*
   other fruit

In a blender, combine the first four ingredients; cover and process for 1 minute or until smooth. Serve with fruit. Refrigerate leftovers. **Yield:** 2 cups.

   Nutritional Analysis: One 2-tablespoon serving of dip equals 40 calories, 58 mg sodium, 1 mg cholesterol, 8 g carbohydrate, 1 g protein, trace fat. **Diabetic Exchange:** 1/2 starch.

Coconut Fruit Dip

(Pictured above)

Nancy Tanguay, Lakeville, Massachusetts

This fruit dip has a fun pineapple and coconut flavor. I usually serve it with melon slices, strawberries and grapes, but you could use whatever fruit you have on hand. It's a big hit whenever I make it.

✓ Uses less fat, sugar or salt. Includes Nutritional Analysis and Diabetic Exchanges.

1 can (8 ounces) crushed unsweetened pineapple,
   undrained

Creamy Thyme Spread

(Pictured below)

Mary Steiner, West Bend, Wisconsin

This make-ahead cracker spread showcases thyme and garlic. A neighbor who has an herb garden gave me the recipe. It's easy and makes a special appetizer for company.

1 package (8 ounces) cream cheese, softened
1 tablespoon minced fresh thyme *or* 1 teaspoon
   dried thyme
1 tablespoon minced fresh parsley *or* 1 teaspoon
   dried parsley flakes
1 garlic clove, minced
Assorted crackers

In a bowl, combine the cream cheese, thyme, parsley and garlic; mix well. Cover and refrigerate until serving. Serve with assorted crackers. Refrigerate leftovers. **Yield:** about 1 cup.

Ham Salad Spread

(Pictured above)

Marcella Kulp, Quakertown, Pennsylvania

My family has enjoyed this hearty ham salad spread for years. It came to be an expected next-day snack every time we had ham for a special dinner. Recently, I decided to measure the ingredients, write down the recipe and pass it on to my daughter and daughter-in-law.

   3 cups ground fully cooked ham
   1 hard-cooked egg, chopped
   2 tablespoons finely chopped celery
   2 teaspoons finely chopped onion
   2 teaspoons sweet pickle relish
  3/4 cup mayonnaise
   1 tablespoon prepared mustard
Assorted crackers

In a bowl, combine the first five ingredients. Combine mayonnaise and mustard; add to ham mixture and mix well. Refrigerate until serving. Serve with crackers. Refrigerate leftovers. **Yield:** 3 cups.

Hot Macadamia Spread

(Pictured at right)

Naomi Francis, Waukesha, Wisconsin

While my husband was in the Army, I'd get together with other wives for snacks and to exchange favorite recipes. I still enjoy serving this rich spread because most guests can't quite put their finger on the zippy ingredient—horseradish.

   1 package (8 ounces) cream cheese, softened
   2 tablespoons milk
  1/2 cup sour cream
   2 teaspoons prepared horseradish
  1/4 cup finely chopped green pepper
   1 green onion, chopped
  1/2 teaspoon garlic salt

  1/4 teaspoon pepper
  1/2 cup chopped macadamia nuts *or* blanched
     almonds
   2 teaspoons butter
Assorted crackers

In a mixing bowl, beat cream cheese and milk until smooth. Stir in sour cream, horseradish, green pepper, onion, garlic salt and pepper. Spoon into an ungreased shallow 2-cup baking dish; set aside.

In a skillet, saute the nuts in butter for 3-4 minutes or until lightly browned. Sprinkle over the cream cheese mixture. Bake, uncovered, at 350° for 20 minutes. Serve with assorted crackers. Refrigerate leftovers. **Yield:** 6-8 servings.

Creamy Horseradish Dip

Barbara Coleman, Dunbar, West Virginia

In this simple-to-prepare vegetable dip, horseradish shines through without being too overpowering.

> ✓ **Uses less fat, sugar or salt. Includes Nutritional Analysis and Diabetic Exchanges.**

   1 cup mayonnaise
   2 tablespoons prepared horseradish
   1 teaspoon white wine vinegar
  1/2 teaspoon curry powder
  1/2 teaspoon garlic salt *or* 1/4 teaspoon garlic
     powder
  1/2 teaspoon ground mustard
Assorted fresh vegetables

In a bowl, combine the first six ingredients. Cover and chill for at least 1 hour. Serve with vegetables. Refrigerate leftovers. **Yield:** about 1 cup.

   Nutritional Analysis: One 2-tablespoon serving (prepared with fat-free mayonnaise and garlic powder) equals 23 calories, 214 mg sodium, 0 cholesterol, 5 g carbohydrate, trace protein, trace fat. **Diabetic Exchange:** 1 vegetable.

Strawberry Fruit Dip

(Pictured at right)

Lydia Graf, Norton, Ohio

I got this recipe from my husband's cousin. It's a refreshing treat during the summer months.

- **1 cup sliced fresh strawberries**
- **1/4 cup sour cream**
- **1 tablespoon sugar**
- **1/4 teaspoon vanilla extract**
- **1/2 cup heavy whipping cream**
- **Assorted fresh fruit**

In a blender, combine the strawberries, sour cream, sugar and vanilla. Cover and process until smooth. In a small mixing bowl, beat cream until stiff peaks form. Fold into strawberry mixture. Cover and refrigerate for 1 hour. Serve with fruit. Refrigerate leftovers. **Yield:** 1-1/2 cups.

Mushroom Liver Pate

Linda Rock, Stratford, Wisconsin

It's easy to make this smooth, zippy spread. And it tastes oh, so good!

- **1/4 pound fresh mushrooms, finely chopped**
- **1 tablespoon butter**
- **1 package (8 ounces) braunschweiger**
- **1/2 cup sour cream**
- **1 tablespoon finely chopped green onion**
- **1/2 teaspoon Dijon mustard**
- **Dash cayenne pepper**
- **Minced fresh parsley**

In a skillet, saute mushrooms in butter until tender. Remove from the heat. Stir in the braunschweiger, sour cream, onion, mustard and cayenne; mix well. Press into a 1-1/2-cup bowl lined with plastic wrap. Cover and refrigerate until serving. Invert onto a plate; garnish with parsley. **Yield:** 1-1/2 cups.

Hearty Nacho Dip

(Pictured below left)

V. Eleanor Dargo, Chapel Hill, North Carolina

This hearty dip is very filling! It's packed with fresh ingredients like green chilies, avocados, tomatoes, onions and more.

- **1 can (16 ounces) refried beans**
- **1 can (4 ounces) chopped green chilies, drained**
- **1-1/2 teaspoons chili powder, *divided***
- **2 teaspoons ground cumin, *divided***
- **2 ripe avocados, peeled and pitted**
- **1/2 cup finely chopped onion, *divided***
- **2 teaspoons lemon juice**
- **1/2 teaspoon sugar**
- **1/2 teaspoon celery salt**
- **1/8 teaspoon cayenne pepper**
- **2 cups salsa, *divided***
- **1 cup (8 ounces) sour cream**
- **1 cup mayonnaise**
- **2 teaspoons paprika**
- **1/2 teaspoon garlic powder**
- **1/2 teaspoon hot pepper sauce**
- **1/4 teaspoon dried oregano**
- **1 cup (4 ounces) shredded Monterey Jack cheese**
- **1 cup (4 ounces) shredded cheddar cheese**
- **2 packages (8 ounces *each*) cream cheese, softened**
- **Chopped green onions and tomatoes**
- **Tortilla chips *or* raw vegetables**

In a bowl, combine the refried beans, chilies, 1 teaspoon chili powder and 1 teaspoon cumin; mix well. Spread over a 14-in. platter. In another bowl, mash the avocados; add 1/4 cup onion, lemon juice, sugar, celery salt and cayenne. Spread over the bean layer.

Combine 1 cup salsa, sour cream, mayonnaise, paprika, garlic powder, pepper sauce, oregano, and remaining onion, cumin and chili powder; mix well. Spread over avocado layer; sprinkle with Monterey Jack and cheddar cheese. In a mixing bowl, beat the cream cheese until smooth. Add the remaining salsa. Spread over cheeses.

Sprinkle with the green onions and tomatoes. Cover and refrigerate until serving. Serve with chips or vegetables. Refrigerate leftovers. **Yield:** 20-25 servings.

Crunchy Vegetable Dip

(Pictured below)

Dottie Miller, Jonesborough, Tennessee

I love to try new recipes, and this one was a big hit with my family. It's great as an appetizer or for a light lunch.

> 1 package (8 ounces) cream cheese, softened
> 1 tablespoon mayonnaise
> 1 tablespoon lemon juice
> 1/2 teaspoon salt
> 1/8 teaspoon pepper
> 3/4 cup grated carrots
> 1/2 cup diced celery
> 1/2 cup diced cucumber
> 1/2 cup diced green pepper
> 1/3 cup diced green onions
> Crackers *or* bread

In a mixing bowl, beat cream cheese, mayonnaise, lemon juice, salt and pepper until smooth. Stir in vegetables. Cover and refrigerate for 2-3 hours. Serve with crackers or use as a sandwich spread. Refrigerate leftovers. **Yield:** about 2 cups.

Mock Guacamole

Diane Molberg, Emerald Park, Saskatchewan

This tempting mixture is a light alternative to traditional guacamole. No one will guess the secret ingredient is peas.

✓ Uses less fat, sugar or salt. Includes Nutritional Analysis and Diabetic Exchanges.

> 1-1/2 cups frozen peas
> 2 tablespoons water
> 1/3 cup fat-free sour cream
> 2 tablespoons mashed ripe avocado
> 1 tablespoon lemon juice
> 1 garlic clove, minced

> 1/2 teaspoon ground cumin
> Dash hot pepper sauce
> 1/2 cup chopped tomato
> 2 tablespoons finely chopped onion
> Raw vegetables *or* baked tortilla chips

Place peas and water in a saucepan; cook for about 2 minutes or until heated through. Drain; place peas in a food processor or blender. Add sour cream, avocado, lemon juice, garlic, cumin and hot pepper sauce; cover and process until smooth. Stir in tomato and onion. Cover and refrigerate for 1 hour. Serve with vegetables or tortilla chips. Refrigerate leftovers. **Yield:** 1-2/3 cups.

Nutritional Analysis: 2 tablespoons of dip equals 25 calories, 25 mg sodium, trace cholesterol, 4 g carbohydrate, 1 g protein, trace fat. **Diabetic Exchange:** 1 vegetable.

Party Crab Dip

Kimberly McGuire, Dunlap, Illinois

Nothing shaves time from party preparations like a no-fuss appetizer. This rich and flavorful seafood spread is the perfect example. Serve it with crackers or toasted bread rounds.

> 1 teaspoon cornstarch
> 1/2 cup white wine *or* chicken broth
> 1 package (8 ounces) cream cheese, cubed
> 2 cans (6 ounces *each*) crabmeat, drained, flaked and cartilage removed
> 2 tablespoons half-and-half cream
> 2 tablespoons minced fresh parsley
> 1 tablespoon Worcestershire sauce
> 1 cup (4 ounces) shredded cheddar cheese
> Seafood seasoning *or* paprika, optional
> Crackers *and/or* raw vegetables

In a microwave-safe bowl, combine the cornstarch and the wine or broth until smooth. Add cream cheese. Cover and microwave on high for 1 minute; stir. Microwave 1 to 1-1/2 minutes longer or until smooth and slightly thickened.

Stir in crab, cream, parsley and Worcestershire sauce. Cover; microwave on high for 1 minute; stir. Add cheddar cheese; heat 1 minute longer. Stir until cheese is melted. Sprinkle with seafood seasoning if desired. Serve with crackers and/or vegetables. Refrigerate leftovers. **Yield:** about 3 cups.

Editor's Note: This recipe was tested in an 850-watt microwave.

Veggie Advice

Tenderize firm vegetable dippers such as broccoli, green beans and cauliflower by placing them in boiling water for a minute or two to cook partially. They should still remain crisp. After blanching, immediately plunge the vegetables in ice water to stop the cooking. Drain well.

Creamy Swiss Spinach Dip

(Pictured above)

Heather Millican, Fort Myers, Florida

A few items and a microwave oven are all you need to throw together this warm cheesy dip. It's always gone at the party's end. My favorite way to serve the dip is in a bread bowl with bread cubes, but it's also good with tortilla chips or French bread slices.

> 1 package (8 ounces) cream cheese, softened
> 1 teaspoon garlic powder
> 1 package (9 ounces) frozen creamed spinach, thawed
> 2 cups diced Swiss cheese
> 2 unsliced round loaves (1 pound *each*) Italian *or* French bread

In a small microwave-safe mixing bowl, beat cream cheese and garlic powder until smooth. Stir in spinach and Swiss cheese. Cover; microwave on high for 5-8 minutes or until cheese is melted, stirring occasionally.

Meanwhile, cut a 4-in. circle in the center of one loaf of bread. Remove bread, leaving 1 in. at bottom of loaf. Cut removed bread and the second loaf into 1-1/2-in. cubes. Spoon hot spinach dip into bread shell. Serve with bread cubes. **Yield:** 3-1/2 cups.

Editor's Note: This recipe was tested in an 850-watt microwave.

Cheddar–Bacon Dip

(Pictured at left)

Carol Werkman, Neerlandia, Alberta

Both children and adults enjoy this dip. I like it, too—it's so quick and easy to prepare. I make it for special occasions …birthdays, Christmastime parties, etc.

> 1 package (8 ounces) cream cheese, softened
> 1 cup (8 ounces) sour cream
> 5 green onions, thinly sliced
> 4 medium tomatoes, chopped
> 1 large green pepper, chopped
> 1 jar (16 ounces) taco sauce
> 2 cups (8 ounces) shredded cheddar cheese
> 1 pound sliced bacon, cooked and crumbled

Tortilla *or* taco chips

In a mixing bowl, beat cream cheese and sour cream. Spread in an ungreased 13-in. x 9-in. x 2-in. dish or on a 12-in. plate. Combine onions, tomatoes and green pepper; sprinkle over the cream cheese layer. Pour taco sauce over the vegetables. Sprinkle with cheddar cheese. Refrigerate. Just before serving, sprinkle with bacon. Serve with tortilla or taco chips. Refrigerate leftovers. **Yield:** 10-12 servings.

Molded Shrimp Spread

(Pictured below)

Mrs. Austin Locke, Prineville, Oregon

I usually make this recipe for parties and family gatherings. It never lasts long because folks go straight for it.

- 1 can (10-3/4 ounces) condensed cream of mushroom soup, undiluted
- 1 package (8 ounces) cream cheese, cubed
- 1 envelope unflavored gelatin
- 3 tablespoons cold water
- 1 cup finely chopped celery
- 1 cup mayonnaise
- 3 tablespoons lemon juice
- 4 green onions, finely chopped
- 1/2 pound cooked shrimp, peeled, deveined and coarsely chopped

Lettuce leaves and additional shrimp, optional
Assorted crackers

In a saucepan, heat soup and cream cheese over medium heat until cheese is melted, stirring frequently. Remove from the heat; set aside to cool.

In a small microwave-safe bowl, sprinkle gelatin over water; let stand for 1 minute. Microwave on high for 40 seconds; stir. Let stand for 2 minutes or until gelatin is completely dissolved. Stir the gelatin mixture, celery, mayonnaise, lemon juice and onions into soup mixture. Fold in shrimp.

Pour into a 5-cup ring mold coated with nonstick cooking spray. Cover and refrigerate for 8 hours or until set. Invert onto a serving plate. Fill center with lettuce and shrimp if desired. Serve with crackers. Refrigerate leftovers. **Yield:** 4-1/4 cups.

- 1 package (8 ounces) cream cheese, softened
- 2 tablespoons sour cream
- 1 to 2 teaspoons curry powder
- 1/2 cup sliced green onions with tops
- 1/2 cup chopped peanuts
- 1 bottle (9 ounces) chutney

Assorted crackers

In a small mixing bowl, beat cream cheese, sour cream and curry powder until smooth. Fold in onions and peanuts. Spread about 1/2 in. thick on a serving plate. Chill. Just before serving, pour chutney over all. Serve with crackers. Refrigerate leftovers. **Yield:** 1-1/2 cups.

Chutney Cracker Spread

Carolyn Eastham, South Bend, Washington

This savory spread on crackers is a delicious alternative to the usual cheese spread.

Garden Salsa

(Pictured above)

Barbara Mundy, Radford, Virginia

I grow almost all of these ingredients in my garden. This recipe makes a large batch, but it's always gone in no time.

- 4 to 5 medium tomatoes, chopped
- 1 medium onion, chopped
- 1 medium green pepper, chopped
- 2 jalapeno peppers, seeded and chopped*
- 2 to 3 tablespoons chopped stuffed olives
- 2 tablespoons minced fresh basil
- 2 tablespoons minced fresh parsley
- 1 can (8 ounces) tomato sauce
- 2 tablespoons olive oil
- 4 teaspoons lime juice
- 1-1/2 teaspoons garlic salt
- 1/2 teaspoon pepper

Tortilla chips

In a bowl, combine the first seven ingredients. In another bowl, combine the tomato sauce, oil, lime juice, garlic salt and pepper. Pour over vegetable mixture and mix well. Cover and refrigerate until serving. Serve with tortilla chips. **Yield:** 7 cups.

***Editor's Note:** When cutting or seeding hot peppers, use rubber or plastic gloves to protect your hands. Avoid touching your face.

 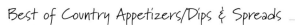

Fruit Salsa

Florence Buchkowsky, Prince Albert, Saskatchewan

My son and I experimented with different ingredients to find the combination we liked best. Using the slow cooker minimizes prep time and maximizes flavor.

> 1 can (11 ounces) mandarin oranges, undrained
> 1 can (8-1/2 ounces) sliced peaches, undrained
> 1 can (8 ounces) pineapple tidbits, undrained
> 1 medium onion, chopped
> 1/2 *each* medium green, sweet red and yellow pepper, chopped
> 3 garlic cloves, minced
> 3 tablespoons cornstarch
> 4 teaspoons vinegar

Tortilla chips

In a slow cooker, combine the fruit, onion, peppers, garlic, cornstarch and vinegar; stir well. Cover and cook on high for 2 hours or until thickened and heated through, stirring occasionally. Serve with tortilla chips. **Yield:** 4 cups.

Bacon-Broccoli Cheese Ball

(Pictured above)

Tamara Rickard, Bartlett, Tennessee

Needing a quick appetizer one night when dinner was running late, I combined a few leftovers into this easy cheese ball. For variety, you can shape it into a log or substitute your favorite herbs for the pepper.

> 1 package (8 ounces) cream cheese, softened
> 1 cup (4 ounces) finely shredded cheddar cheese
> 1/2 teaspoon pepper
> 1 cup finely chopped broccoli florets
> 6 bacon strips, cooked and crumbled

Assorted crackers

In a mixing bowl, beat cream cheese, cheddar cheese and pepper until blended. Stir in broccoli. Shape into a ball and roll in bacon. Cover and refrigerate. Remove from the refrigerator 15 minutes before serving. Serve with crackers. Refrigerate leftovers. **Yield:** 2-1/2 cups.

Cool Cucumber Dip

Gail Rhoades, Denver, Colorado

You can whip up this creamy dip in your food processor in no time, then chill it 'til company comes. The garden-fresh flavor of the cucumber really complements the vegetable dippers. Be sure to tell your guests to save room for the main course!

> 1/2 small cucumber, peeled, seeded and cubed
> 1 small onion, chopped
> 1 package (8 ounces) cream cheese, cubed
> 1/2 cup mayonnaise
> 1/2 to 1 teaspoon celery seed
> 1/2 teaspoon garlic salt
> 2 to 3 tablespoons Western salad dressing

Fresh vegetables

Combine first seven ingredients in a blender or food processor; cover and process until smooth. Chill. Serve with vegetables. Refrigerate leftovers. **Yield:** 2 cups.

Sweet 'n' Hot Mustard Dip

(Pictured at right)

Rita Reifenstein, Evans City, Pennsylvania

With pretzels, this sweet and spicy mustard is a fun snack. It also sparks the flavor of grilled chicken strips or sausages.

> 1-1/2 cups honey
> 1 cup vinegar
> 3 eggs
> 2 containers (1-3/4 ounces *each*) ground mustard
> 1/2 teaspoon salt

Pretzels, cooked chicken fingers *or* sausage slices

In a blender, combine the first five ingredients; cover and process until blended. Pour into a saucepan; cook and stir over low heat until mixture thickens and reaches 160°. Pour into small jars. Cover and refrigerate for up to 1 week. Serve with pretzels, chicken fingers or sausage. **Yield:** 2-1/3 cups.

Pineapple Cheese Spread

Cindy Smith, Adel, Iowa

This satisfying snack is a real treat for my husband, who's watching his weight. Crushed pineapple adds a hint of sweetness to my low-fat version of a spread sold at a grocery store chain.

 Uses less fat, sugar or salt. Includes Nutritional Analysis and Diabetic Exchanges.

2 green onions, chopped
1/2 cup shredded reduced-fat cheddar cheese
1/2 cup shredded part-skim mozzarella cheese
1/4 cup unsweetened crushed pineapple
1/3 cup fat-free mayonnaise
Reduced-fat crackers

In a bowl, combine first five ingredients; mix well. Cover; refrigerate for 30 minutes or until serving. Serve with crackers. Refrigerate leftovers. **Yield:** 1 cup.
Nutritional Analysis: One 1/4-cup serving (calculated without crackers) equals 100 calories, 5 g fat (3 g saturated fat), 16 mg cholesterol, 258 mg sodium, 7 g carbohydrate, trace fiber, 9 g protein. **Diabetic Exchanges:** 1 lean meat, 1 fat.

Warm Olive Dip

Cindy Armstrong, Porterville, California

We grow olives and like to utilize them in a variety of recipes. I use them in everything from egg dishes to appetizers like this savory dip.

1-1/4 cups mayonnaise
1 cup shredded *or* grated Parmesan cheese
1 can (14 ounces) water-packed artichoke hearts, drained and chopped
1 cup pimiento-stuffed *or* any spiced olive, chopped
Assorted crackers

In a bowl, combine the mayonnaise and Parmesan cheese. Add artichokes and olives; mix well. Transfer to an ungreased 1-qt. baking dish. Bake, uncovered, at 350° for 30 minutes or until bubbly. Serve with crackers. Refrigerate leftovers. **Yield:** 3 cups.

Baked Onion Dip

Mona Zignego, Hartford, Wisconsin

Some people like this cheesy dip so much that they can't tear themselves away from the appetizer table to eat their dinner.

1 cup mayonnaise
1 cup chopped sweet onion
1 tablespoon grated Parmesan cheese
1/4 teaspoon garlic salt
1 cup (4 ounces) shredded Swiss cheese
Minced fresh parsley, optional
Assorted crackers

In a bowl, combine mayonnaise, onion, Parmesan cheese and garlic salt; stir in Swiss cheese. Spoon into a 1-qt.

baking dish. Bake, uncovered, at 325° for 40 minutes. Sprinkle with parsley if desired. Serve with crackers. Refrigerate leftovers. **Yield:** 2 cups.

Hot Artichoke Spread

(Pictured above)
Victoria Casey, Coeur d'Alene, Idaho

Green chilies add a bit of zip to this rich cracker spread. I serve this appetizer often because it's tasty, quick to make and looks so pretty with the red tomatoes and green onions on top.

1 can (14 ounces) water-packed artichoke hearts, drained and chopped
1 cup mayonnaise*
1 cup grated Parmesan cheese
1 can (4 ounces) chopped green chilies, drained
1 garlic clove, minced
1 cup chopped fresh tomatoes
3 green onions, thinly sliced
Crackers *or* pita bread

In a bowl, combine the first five ingredients. Spread into a 1-qt. baking dish or 9-in. pie plate. Bake, uncovered, at 350° for 20-25 minutes or until top is lightly browned. Sprinkle with tomatoes and onions. Serve with crackers or pita bread. Refrigerate leftovers. **Yield:** 4-1/2 cups.
Editor's Note: Reduced-fat or fat-free mayonnaise may not be substituted for regular mayonnaise.

Shaping a Cheese Ball

To keep hands and countertop clean, spoon the cheese mixture onto a piece of plastic wrap. Working from the underside of the wrap, pat the mixture into a ball. Complete the recipe as directed.

1 can (4 ounces) chopped green chilies, drained
1 envelope taco seasoning
1/2 cup chopped onion
Tortilla chips

In a slow cooker, combine the first eight ingredients. Cover and cook on low for 5-7 hours. Serve with tortilla chips. **Yield:** about 7 cups.

Cucumber Dill Spread

(Pictured below)

Doris Heath, Bryson City, North Carolina

For a delightfully different way to serve cucumbers, try this spread. It's so good with crackers or vegetables.

✓ Uses less fat, sugar or salt. Includes Nutritional Analysis and Diabetic Exchanges.

2 packages (8 ounces *each*) cream cheese, softened
2 teaspoons lemon juice
2 teaspoons minced onion
1/2 teaspoon dill weed
1/4 teaspoon prepared horseradish
Dash hot pepper sauce
3/4 cup finely diced seeded cucumber
Fresh vegetables *or* crackers

In a mixing bowl, beat cream cheese until smooth. Add lemon juice, onion, dill, horseradish and hot pepper sauce. Fold in cucumber. Cover and chill for at least 1 hour. Serve with crackers or raw vegetables. Refrigerate leftovers. **Yield:** 2-1/3 cups.

Nutritional Analysis: 2 tablespoons (prepared with fat-free cream cheese) equals 45 calories, 240 mg sodium, 0 cholesterol, 4 g carbohydrate, 7 g protein, 0 fat.
Diabetic Exchanges: 1 vegetable, 1/2 very lean meat.

Taco Joe Dip

(Pictured above)

Lang Secrest, Sierra Vista, Arizona

This recipe was given to us by our daughter. Because it's made in a slow cooker, it's great for parties or busy days.

1 can (16 ounces) kidney beans, rinsed and drained
1 can (15-1/4 ounces) whole kernel corn, drained
1 can (15 ounces) black beans, rinsed and drained
1 can (14-1/2 ounces) stewed tomatoes
1 can (8 ounces) tomato sauce

1 pound bulk Italian sausage
1 can (10 ounces) diced tomatoes and green chilies, drained
1 package (8 ounces) cream cheese, cubed
Assorted crackers

In a skillet, cook sausage over medium heat until no longer pink; drain. Stir in the tomatoes and cream cheese; cook until cheese is melted. Serve warm with crackers. Refrigerate leftovers. **Yield:** 3 cups.

Corn and Bacon Dip

(Pictured below)

Carolyn Zaschak, Corning, New York

The recipe for this creamy appetizer was given to me about 20 years ago. I've made it many times since then, and it becomes a favorite wherever I share it.

1 package (8 ounces) cream cheese, softened
1 cup (8 ounces) sour cream
1/4 cup mayonnaise
2 garlic cloves, minced
1/4 teaspoon hot pepper sauce
1 can (15-1/4 ounces) whole kernel corn, drained
8 bacon strips, cooked and crumbled
Assorted raw vegetables *and/or* crackers

In a mixing bowl, combine the first five ingredients. Stir in corn and bacon. Cover and refrigerate for several hours. Serve with vegetables and/or crackers. Refrigerate leftovers. **Yield:** 3 cups.

Salsa Guacamole

(Pictured above)
Lauren Heyn, Oak Creek, Wisconsin

I've never tasted better guacamole than this. If there's time, I make homemade tortilla chips by frying 1-inch strips of flour tortillas in oil and salting them.

> ✓ Uses less fat, sugar or salt. Includes Nutritional Analysis and Diabetic Exchanges.

6 small ripe avocados, halved, pitted and peeled
1/4 cup lemon juice
1 cup salsa
2 green onions, finely chopped
1/4 teaspoon salt *or* salt-free seasoning blend
1/4 teaspoon garlic powder
Tortilla chips

In a bowl, mash avocados with lemon juice. Stir in the salsa, onions, salt and garlic powder. Serve immediately with tortilla chips. **Yield:** 4 cups.

Nutritional Analysis: 2 tablespoons (prepared with salt-free seasoning blend; calculated without tortilla chips) equals 10 calories, 55 mg sodium, 0 cholesterol, 1 g carbohydrate, trace protein, 1 g fat. **Diabetic Exchange:** Free food.

Zippy Sausage Spread

Bridget Miller, Colorado Springs, Colorado

I always keep the ingredients for this zesty appetizer on hand. It's quick, hearty and delicious. I serve it from my slow cooker so it stays warm during parties.

Spinach Dip in a Bread Bowl

(Pictured at right)

Janelle Lee, Sulphur, Louisiana

We often get together with friends. I like to prepare this creamy dip. It's a crowd-pleaser.

    2 cups (16 ounces) sour cream
    1 envelope ranch salad dressing mix
    1 package (10 ounces) frozen chopped spinach,
       thawed and well drained
    1/4 cup chopped onion
    3/4 teaspoon dried basil
    1/2 teaspoon dried oregano
    1 round loaf of bread (1 pound)
Raw vegetables

In a bowl, combine first six ingredients. Chill for at least 1 hour. Cut a 1-1/2-in. slice off the top of the loaf; set aside. Hollow out the bottom part, leaving a thick shell.

Cut or tear the slice from the top of the loaf and the bread from inside into bite-size pieces. Fill the shell with dip; set on a large platter. Arrange the bread pieces and vegetables around it and serve immediately. **Yield:** 10-15 servings.

Cheddar Fondue

(Pictured below and on front cover)

Norene Wright, Manilla, Indiana

This cheesy blend, sparked with mustard and Worcestershire sauce, is yummy.

    1/4 cup butter
    1/4 cup all-purpose flour
    1/2 teaspoon salt, optional
    1/4 teaspoon pepper
    1/4 teaspoon ground mustard
    1/4 teaspoon Worcestershire sauce
  1-1/2 cups milk
    2 cups (8 ounces) shredded cheddar cheese
Bread cubes, ham cubes, bite-size sausage *and/or* broccoli florets

In a saucepan, melt butter; stir in flour, salt if desired, pepper, mustard and Worcestershire sauce until smooth. Gradually add milk. Bring to a boil; cook and stir for 2 minutes or until thickened. Reduce heat. Add the cheese; cook and stir until melted. Transfer to a fondue pot or slow cooker; keep warm. Serve with bread, ham, sausage and/or broccoli. **Yield:** 2-1/2 cups.

Garlic Dip

Jauneen Hosking, Wind Lake, Wisconsin

I've been making this dip for years, and now my grown daughters fix it for their families. My mom makes it, too, and her motto is, "You can never have too much garlic".

✓ Uses less fat, sugar or salt. Includes Nutritional Analysis and Diabetic Exchanges.

    1 package (8 ounces) cream cheese, softened
    1/2 cup sour cream
    1 tablespoon milk
  1-1/2 teaspoons Worcestershire sauce
    3 garlic cloves, minced
    1/4 teaspoon salt
    1/8 teaspoon pepper
Fresh vegetables *and/or* pretzels

In a small mixing bowl, beat the cream cheese, sour cream, milk, Worcestershire sauce, garlic, salt and pepper. Serve with vegetables and/or pretzels. Refrigerate leftovers. **Yield:** 1-1/2 cups.

Nutritional Analysis: 1/4 cup of dip (prepared with fat-free cream cheese and reduced-fat sour cream) equals 68 calories, 2 g fat (2 g saturated fat), 10 mg cholesterol, 333 mg sodium, 4 g carbohydrate, trace fiber, 7 g protein. **Diabetic Exchange:** 1/2 fat-free milk.

Venison Cheese Dip

(Pictured at right)

Karen Smith, Mackinaw, Illinois

This hearty cheesy dip is so yummy that even those who don't enjoy venison will dig right in. My grandsons put it in a bowl and eat it with a spoon!

    1 pound ground venison
3/4 cup chopped onion, *divided*
3/4 cup chopped green pepper, *divided*
    2 tablespoons vegetable oil
    1 pound process cheese (Velveeta), cubed
    1 can (15 ounces) chili without beans
    1 bottle (12 ounces) chili sauce
1/2 teaspoon garlic salt
1/2 teaspoon salt
1/2 teaspoon pepper
1/2 cup shredded cheddar cheese
Nacho chips

In a large skillet over medium heat, cook the venison, 1/2 cup onion and 1/2 cup green pepper in oil until meat is no longer pink; drain. Stir in the next six ingredients; cook and stir until the cheese is melted. Transfer to a serving dish. Sprinkle with cheddar cheese and remaining onion and green pepper. Serve with chips. Refrigerate leftovers. **Yield:** 6 cups.

Herbed Garlic Cheese Spread

(Pictured below)

Christine Duffy, Concord, New Hampshire

I've taken this creamy spread to many holiday gatherings and parties—and there's never any left to bring home!

    2 packages (8 ounces *each*) cream cheese, softened
    1 cup butter, softened

1/2 teaspoon *each* dried basil, marjoram, oregano, thyme, dill weed, garlic powder and pepper
Assorted crackers

In a mixing bowl, beat the cream cheese, butter and seasonings until well blended. Cover and refrigerate for at least 2 hours. Serve with crackers. Refrigerate leftovers. **Yield:** about 3 cups.

Tomato Eggplant Salsa

Anna Free, Plymouth, Ohio

Eggplant and a zippy combination of peppers, herbs and seasonings make this unique salsa a real crowd-pleaser.

    3/4 cup water
    1 small sweet red pepper, chopped
    1 celery rib, chopped
    2 jalapeno peppers, seeded and minced*
    2 garlic cloves, minced
    1 bay leaf
    2 teaspoons minced fresh thyme *or* 1/2 teaspoon dried thyme, *divided*
    1 teaspoon hot pepper sauce
1-1/2 cups cubed eggplant
1/4 cup plus 1 tablespoon olive oil, *divided*
    5 plum tomatoes, chopped
    3 green onions, cut into 1-inch strips
1/2 teaspoon salt

In a saucepan, combine first six ingredients, half of the thyme and hot pepper sauce. Bring to a boil. Reduce heat; simmer, uncovered, for 15 minutes or until liquid is evaporated. Remove from heat; discard bay leaf.

In a skillet, saute eggplant in 1/4 cup oil until tender. Transfer to a bowl. Add red pepper mixture, tomatoes, onions, salt and remaining thyme and oil; mix well. Cover and refrigerate until serving. **Yield:** about 2-1/2 cups.

*Editor's Note: When cutting or seeding hot peppers, use rubber or plastic gloves to protect your hands. Avoid touching your face.

Reuben Spread

(Pictured above)

Rosalie Fuchs, Paynesville, Minnesota

I received the recipe for this hearty spread from my daughter. Whenever I serve it at parties, everyone agrees it tastes just like a Reuben sandwich. I keep the slow cooker plugged in while serving it, so it stays warm.

    1 jar (16 ounces) sauerkraut, rinsed and drained
    1 package (8 ounces) cream cheese, cubed
    2 cups (8 ounces) shredded Swiss cheese
    1 package (3 ounces) deli corned beef, chopped
    3 tablespoons Thousand Island salad dressing
Snack rye bread *or* crackers

In a 1-1/2-qt. slow cooker, combine the first five ingredients. Cover and cook for 2 hours or until cheeses are melted; stir to blend. Serve warm with bread or crackers. Refrigerate leftovers. **Yield:** 3-1/2 cups.

Pumpkin Cheese Ball

Linnea Rein, Topeka, Kansas

No one will guess that this make-ahead spread has pumpkin in it, but that subtle ingredient lends harvest color and added nutrition.

    1 package (8 ounces) cream cheese, softened
1/2 cup canned pumpkin
    1 can (8 ounces) crushed pineapple, well drained
    2 cups (8 ounces) shredded sharp cheddar cheese
    1 package (2-1/2 ounces) dried beef, finely chopped
    1 tablespoon finely chopped onion

Celery leaves
Crackers *and/or* raw vegetables

In a mixing bowl, beat cream cheese, pumpkin and pineapple. Stir in cheddar cheese, beef and onion. Shape into a ball; place on a serving platter. Score sides with a knife to resemble a pumpkin and add celery leaves for a stem. Serve with crackers and/or vegetables. Refrigerate leftovers. **Yield:** 3 cups.

Mustard Egg Dip

Janie Carr, Fort Davis, Texas

I especially like to make this dip around Easter, when I have plenty of hard-cooked eggs on hand. The zippy blend tastes delicious served with a variety of fresh vegetables.

    6 hard-cooked eggs, finely chopped
1/3 cup mayonnaise
    1 tablespoon butter, softened
    2 teaspoons lemon juice
    1 teaspoon prepared mustard
    1 teaspoon Worcestershire sauce
3/4 teaspoon Liquid Smoke, optional
1/2 teaspoon salt
1/4 teaspoon pepper
Hot pepper sauce to taste
Green *or* sweet red peppers and other raw vegetables

In a bowl, combine the first 10 ingredients and mix until smooth. Serve dip with sliced peppers and other raw vegetables, or, if desired, cut the peppers in half lengthwise and fill with the dip. Refrigerate leftovers. **Yield:** 1-3/4 cups.

Turkey Taco Dip

(Pictured at right)

Liz Adcock, Rayville, Louisiana

I created this zippy snack when I had a craving for tacos, but didn't want all the fat and calories that go along with them. It's quick to fix and uses ingredients I usually have on hand.

✓ **Uses less fat, sugar or salt. Includes Nutritional Analysis and Diabetic Exchanges.**

- 1 pound ground turkey breast
- 1 envelope reduced-sodium taco seasoning
- 1 cup water
- 1 package (8 ounces) fat-free cream cheese, softened
- 1 cup (8 ounces) fat-free sour cream
- 3/4 cup picante sauce
- 1/2 cup shredded lettuce
- 1 cup chopped fresh tomato
- 1 cup (4 ounces) shredded fat-free cheddar cheese

Baked tortilla chips

In a skillet, cook turkey over medium heat until no longer pink; drain. Add taco seasoning and water; cover and simmer for 10 minutes. Spoon turkey onto a 12-in. serving plate or pizza pan. In a mixing bowl, beat the cream cheese until smooth. Add sour cream; spread over the meat mixture. Spread with picante sauce. Top with lettuce, tomato and cheese. Serve with tortilla chips. Refrigerate leftovers. **Yield:** 10 servings.

Nutritional Analysis: One serving (calculated without chips) equals 135 calories, 569 mg sodium, 18 mg cholesterol, 11 g carbohydrate, 19 g protein, 1 g fat, trace fiber. **Diabetic Exchanges:** 2 very lean meat, 1 vegetable, 1/2 starch.

Salmon Party Spread

(Pictured below left)

Kathy Crow, Cordova, Alaska

This recipe deliciously showcases our state's flavorful salmon. Guests love it!

- 1 package (8 ounces) cream cheese, softened
- 1 can (7-1/2 ounces) pink salmon, drained, flaked and cartilage removed
- 3 tablespoons chopped fresh parsley
- 2 tablespoons finely chopped green pepper
- 2 tablespoons finely chopped sweet red pepper
- 2 teaspoons grated onion
- 1 teaspoon lemon juice
- 1 teaspoon prepared horseradish
- 1/2 teaspoon Liquid Smoke, optional

Finely chopped pecans *or* additional parsley
Crackers

In a bowl, combine the first nine ingredients; stir until well blended. Cover and chill for 2 to 24 hours. Transfer to a serving bowl; sprinkle with pecans or parsley. Serve with crackers. Refrigerate leftovers. **Yield:** 2 cups.

Take the Chill Off

Allow cheese balls, dips and spreads that contain cream cheese to stand at room temperature 15 minutes before serving for easier spreading and more flavor.

Black Bean Salsa

(Pictured at right)

Charlene Denges, Elgin, Texas

This sensational salsa is a colorful combination of lots of fresh-tasting flavors. My husband, son and I think it's great. We love taste-testing my creations together.

    2 cans (15 ounces *each*) black beans, rinsed
      and drained
    1 can (15-1/4 ounces) whole kernel corn, drained
    1 can (10 ounces) diced tomatoes and green
      chilies, undrained
    1 jar (7-1/2 ounces) roasted red peppers,
      drained and diced
    2 plum tomatoes, chopped
    1 medium red onion, finely chopped
    4 green onions, finely chopped
  2/3 cup minced fresh cilantro
    2 garlic cloves, minced
  1/3 cup orange juice
    1 teaspoon ground cumin
    1 teaspoon grated orange peel
  1/8 teaspoon coarsely ground pepper
Tortilla chips

In a large bowl, combine the first 13 ingredients. Cover and refrigerate for at least 2 hours. Serve with tortilla chips. Refrigerate leftovers. **Yield:** 8 cups.

Roasted Garlic Spread

Janice Mitchell, Aurora, Colorado

Since garlic is so easy to grow, it's one of the favorite plants in our garden. This thick spread has a mild, mellow flavor.

    2 large garlic heads
    1 teaspoon olive oil
    1 to 2 tablespoons butter
    1 to 2 tablespoons all-purpose flour
    1 teaspoon chicken bouillon granules
  2/3 cup boiling water
Italian *or* French bread, sliced

Remove papery outer skin from garlic (do not peel or separate cloves). Brush with oil. Wrap each head in heavy-duty aluminum foil. Bake at 425° for 30-35 minutes or until softened. Cool for 10-15 minutes. Cut top off garlic heads, leaving root end intact.

In a small saucepan, melt butter. Squeeze softened garlic into pan. Stir in flour until blended. Dissolve bouillon in water; gradually add to garlic mixture. Bring to a boil; cook and stir for 2 minutes. Serve with bread. **Yield:** about 1/2 cup.

Fiesta Dip

(Pictured below left)

Rhonda Cowden, Quincy, Illinois

I sprinkle a warm creamy bean mixture with colorful toppings to create an effortless appetizer.

    2 cups (16 ounces) sour cream
    1 can (16 ounces) refried beans
    1 can (4 ounces) chopped green chilies *or*
      jalapenos
    1 envelope fiesta ranch dip mix
    2 cups (8 ounces) shredded Mexican cheese blend
      or cheddar cheese, *divided*
Sliced ripe olives, chopped tomatoes, sliced green
  onions and shredded lettuce, optional
Tortilla chips

In a shallow 1-1/2-qt. microwave-safe dish, combine the sour cream, beans, chilies and dip mix. Stir in 1 cup cheese. Cover and microwave on high for 3 minutes. Stir; rotate dish a quarter turn. Cover and microwave 2 minutes longer or until heated through. Sprinkle with remaining cheese. Top with olives, tomatoes, onions and lettuce if desired. Serve with tortilla chips. Refrigerate leftovers. **Yield:** about 5 cups.

Editor's Note: This recipe was tested in an 850-watt microwave.

Festive Pumpkin Dip

(Pictured below)

Evelyn Kennell, Roanoke, Illinois

Surprise family and friends with this delicious hors d'oeuvre. It's perfect for the holidays or anytime.

    12 ounces cream cheese, softened
    3/4 cup canned pumpkin
    2 tablespoons taco seasoning mix
    1/8 teaspoon garlic powder
    1/3 cup chopped dried beef
    1/3 cup chopped green pepper
    1/3 cup chopped sweet red pepper
    1 can (2-1/4 ounces) sliced ripe olives, drained
    1 round loaf (1 pound) Italian *or* pumpernickel
      bread
Fresh vegetables, crackers *or* corn chips

In a mixing bowl, beat cream cheese, pumpkin, taco seasoning and garlic powder until smooth. Stir in beef, peppers and olives. Cover and refrigerate until serving.

Just before serving, cut top off bread; scoop out bread from inside, leaving a 1/2-in. shell (save the bread from inside to make croutons or bread crumbs or save for another use). Fill shell with cream cheese mixture. Serve with vegetables, crackers or corn chips. **Yield:** 3 cups.

✓ **Uses less fat, sugar or salt. Includes Nutritional Analysis and Diabetic Exchanges.**

Cinnamon 'n' Spice Dip

(Pictured above right)

Julie Bertha, Pittsburgh, Pennsylvania

Cinnamon, nutmeg and brown sugar dress up whipped topping in this extremely easy party pleaser. My gang especially likes the dip with apples and pears, but feel free to try it with pineapple slices, strawberries and other fresh fruit.

    2 cups whipped topping
    1/4 cup packed brown sugar
    1/8 to 1/4 teaspoon ground cinnamon
Dash ground nutmeg
Assorted fresh fruit

In a small bowl, combine the whipped topping, brown sugar, cinnamon and nutmeg. Serve with fruit. Refrigerate leftovers. **Yield:** about 2 cups.

Nutritional Analysis: 2 tablespoons dip (prepared with reduced-fat whipped topping; calculated without fruit) equals 66 calories, 2 g fat (2 g saturated fat), 0 cholesterol, 3 mg sodium, 11 g carbohydrate, trace fiber, 0 protein. **Diabetic Exchange:** 1/2 starch.

Picadillo Dip

(Pictured above)

Lisa Revell, Vernon, New Jersey

For a hearty hot dip that's both sweet and savory, try this recipe. The unusual combination of ingredients makes this snack great.

- 1 pound ground beef
- 1 cup water
- 1 garlic clove, minced
- 1/2 teaspoon salt
- 1/4 teaspoon pepper
- 1 can (14-1/2 ounces) diced tomatoes, undrained
- 1 can (6 ounces) tomato paste
- 1/2 cup raisins
- 1/2 cup slivered almonds
- 1/4 cup chopped stuffed olives
- 1/2 teaspoon sugar
Tortilla chips

In a large saucepan, cook beef over medium heat until no longer pink. Add water, garlic, salt and pepper. Cover and simmer for 20 minutes; drain. Add next six ingredients; mix well. Cover and simmer for 45 minutes, stirring occasionally. Serve hot with chips. Refrigerate leftovers. **Yield:** 4 cups.

Sweet Potato Cheese Ball

(Pictured at right)

Edwina Harper, Bastrop, Louisiana

My husband and I farm 300 acres of sweet potatoes. This recipe is a great way to use our produce.

- 1 package (8 ounces) cream cheese, softened
- 2 cups cold mashed sweet potatoes

- 1/4 cup finely chopped onion
- 2 tablespoons finely chopped jalapeno pepper*
- 1 teaspoon seasoned salt
- 1 teaspoon Worcestershire sauce
- 1 teaspoon Louisiana hot sauce
- 1/2 to 1 teaspoon hot pepper sauce
- 1/4 cup chopped pecans
Assorted crackers, breadsticks *or* raw vegetables

In a mixing bowl, beat cream cheese and sweet potatoes until smooth. Add the next seven ingredients; mix well. Cover and refrigerate for 4 hours or until easy to handle. Shape into a ball; cover and refrigerate for 4 hours or until firm. Serve with crackers, breadsticks or vegetables. Refrigerate leftovers. **Yield:** about 3 cups.

*Editor's Note:** When cutting or seeding hot peppers, use rubber or plastic gloves to protect your hands. Avoid touching your face.

Chili Con Queso

Patricia Leinheiser, Albuquerque, New Mexico

My husband created this thick, cheesy Southwestern dip by adapting a recipe he found in a cookbook. It's excellent.

- 1 medium onion, chopped
- 1 to 2 garlic cloves, minced
- 2 tablespoons butter
- 1 can (4 ounces) chopped green chilies
- 2-1/2 cups (10 ounces) shredded cheddar cheese
- 2 cups (8 ounces) shredded Monterey Jack cheese
- 1 cup milk
Tortilla chips

In a saucepan, saute onion and garlic in butter until tender. Add chilies; cook and stir for 5 minutes. Reduce heat to low. Gradually add small amounts of cheeses and milk; stir until melted after each addition. Serve warm with tortilla chips. Refrigerate leftovers. **Yield:** 3 cups.

Curry Carrot Dip

Louise Weyer, Marietta, Georgia

The flavors of curry and mustard blend deliciously in this appetizing dip. It's great with an assortment of vegetables.

✓ **Uses less fat, sugar or salt. Includes Nutritional Analysis and Diabetic Exchanges.**

    1 small onion, chopped
    2 teaspoons canola oil
    4 medium carrots, sliced
    1/3 cup water
    1/4 teaspoon salt
    1/4 teaspoon pepper
    1/4 teaspoon curry powder
    2 tablespoons reduced-fat mayonnaise
    2 teaspoons prepared mustard
Assorted raw vegetables

In a nonstick skillet, saute onion in oil. Add the carrots, water, salt, pepper and curry. Bring to a boil. Reduce heat; cover and simmer for 6 minutes or until vegetables are tender. Uncover; cook for 8 minutes or until liquid has evaporated. Cool. Transfer to a food processor or blender; cover and process until smooth. Add mayonnaise and mustard; mix well. Serve with vegetables. Refrigerate leftovers. **Yield:** 1 cup.

    Nutritional Analysis: One serving (2 tablespoons dip) equals 45 calories, 2 g fat (trace saturated fat), 1 mg cholesterol, 140 mg sodium, 5 g carbohydrate, 1 g fiber, 1 g protein. **Diabetic Exchange:** 1/2 starch.

Pinto Bean Dip

Claire Rademacher, Whittier, California

Whenever there's a gathering, friends tell me, "Be sure to bring your bean dip!" With several delightful layers, this is more than a snack—some guests practically make a meal out of it. You'll need big chips to pick up all the ingredients.

    1 can (29 ounces) pinto beans, rinsed and drained
1-1/4 teaspoons salt, *divided*
    1/4 teaspoon pepper
    1/8 to 1/4 teaspoon hot pepper sauce
    3 ripe avocados, peeled and pitted
    4 teaspoons lemon juice
    1 cup (8 ounces) sour cream
    1/2 cup mayonnaise
    1 envelope taco seasoning mix
    1 cup sliced green onions
    2 medium tomatoes, chopped
1-1/2 cups (6 ounces) shredded cheddar cheese
    1 can (2-1/4 ounces) sliced ripe olives, drained
Tortilla chips

In a bowl, mash beans with a fork; stir in 3/4 teaspoon salt, pepper and hot pepper sauce. Spread onto a 12-in. serving plate. Mash avocados with lemon juice and remaining salt; spread over bean mixture. Combine sour cream, mayonnaise and taco seasoning; spread over avocado layer. Sprinkle with onions, tomatoes, cheese and olives. Serve with tortilla chips. Refrigerate leftovers. **Yield:** 25-30 servings.

Zippy Cheese Dip

(Pictured above)

Diane Hixon, Niceville, Florida

I first tasted this dip in a cooking class at a local supermarket. It isn't necessary to add the eggs, but they give the dip a thicker consistency.

    1/4 cup chopped onion
    1 tablespoon butter
    1 can (14-1/2 ounces) diced tomatoes, drained
    1 pound process American cheese, cubed
    1 teaspoon Worcestershire sauce
    1/2 teaspoon paprika
    1/4 teaspoon salt
    2 drops hot pepper sauce
    2 eggs, beaten
Crackers

In a saucepan, saute onion in butter until tender. Add tomatoes, cheese, Worcestershire sauce, paprika, salt and hot pepper sauce. Cook and stir over medium heat until cheese is melted. Remove from the heat.

    Stir a small amount of hot mixture into eggs. Return all to the pan, stirring constantly. Cook and stir until mixture reaches 160°. Serve warm with crackers. Refrigerate leftovers. **Yield:** 3-1/2 cups.

Pretty Presentation

For splashes of color, garnish appetizer platters with sprigs of freshly picked herbs, lemon wedges, grape clusters or fresh berries. Line vegetable and dip platters with leaf lettuce.

    In addition to your usual vegetable dippers, try radishes, sweet red pepper strips, sugar snap peas and cherry tomatoes.

Pizza by the Scoop

Georgene Robertson, Pikeville, Kentucky

This tasty cold snack dip is one of my most-requested recipes and always pleases friends at get-togethers. People keep scooping until the platter is clean.

- 2 packages (8 ounces *each*) cream cheese, softened
- 1 bottle (12 ounces) chili sauce
- 1 package (6 ounces) Canadian bacon, chopped
- 1 small onion, chopped
- 1 small green pepper, chopped
- 3/4 cup shredded mozzarella cheese
- 3/4 cup shredded cheddar cheese

Corn chips

Spread cream cheese on an ungreased 12-in. pizza pan. Spread with chili sauce. Sprinkle with Canadian bacon, onion, green pepper and cheeses. Serve with chips. Refrigerate leftovers. **Yield:** 14-16 servings.

Radish Dip

(Pictured below)

Donna Smith, Victor, New York

I put an unusual spin on yogurt dip by adding radishes. This creamy dip makes a zippy appetizer when served with cauliflower and broccoli florets or rye bread cubes.

✓ Uses less fat, sugar or salt. Includes Nutritional Analysis and Diabetic Exchanges.

- 1 cup (8 ounces) fat-free plain yogurt
- 1 cup chopped radishes (about 13)
- 1/3 cup reduced-fat mayonnaise
- 1/4 teaspoon hot pepper sauce
- 1/8 teaspoon pepper

Raw vegetables

In a bowl, combine the first five ingredients; mix well. Cover and refrigerate until serving. Serve with vegetables. Refrigerate leftovers. **Yield:** about 1-1/3 cups.

Nutritional Analysis: One serving (2 tablespoons) equals 29 calories, 1 g fat (trace saturated fat), 2 mg cholesterol, 53 mg sodium, 3 g carbohydrate, trace fiber, 1 g protein. **Diabetic Exchange:** 1 vegetable.

Four-Tomato Salsa

(Pictured above)

Connie Siese, Wayne, Michigan

A variety of tomatoes, onions and peppers makes this chunky salsa so good. Whenever I try to take a batch to a get-together, it's hard to keep my family from finishing it off first! It's a super snack with tortilla chips or as a relish with meat.

✓ Uses less fat, sugar or salt. Includes Nutritional Analysis and Diabetic Exchanges.

- 7 plum tomatoes, chopped
- 7 medium tomatoes, chopped
- 3 medium yellow tomatoes, chopped
- 3 medium orange tomatoes, chopped
- 1 teaspoon salt
- 2 tablespoons lime juice
- 2 tablespoons olive oil
- 1 medium white onion, chopped
- 2/3 cup chopped red onion
- 2 green onions, chopped
- 1/2 cup *each* chopped sweet red, orange, yellow and green pepper
- 3 pepperoncinis, chopped
- 3 pickled sweet banana wax peppers, chopped
- 1/2 cup minced fresh parsley
- 2 tablespoons minced fresh cilantro
- 1 tablespoon dried chervil

Tortilla chips

In a colander, combine the tomatoes and salt. Let drain for 10 minutes. Transfer to a large bowl. Stir in the lime juice, oil, onions, peppers, parsley, cilantro and chervil. Serve with tortilla chips. Refrigerate leftovers. **Yield:** 14 cups.

Nutritional Analysis: One serving (1/4 cup salsa) equals 16 calories, 1 g fat (0 saturated fat), 0 cholesterol, 63 mg sodium, 3 g carbohydrate, 1 g fiber, 1 g protein. **Diabetic Exchange:** Free food.

Editor's Note: Look for pepperoncinis (pickled peppers) and pickled banana peppers in the pickle and olive aisle of your grocery store.

Fiesta Cheese Ball

(Pictured at right)

Virginia Horst, Mesa, Washington

Whenever I bring this zippy cheese ball to church functions, showers and parties, folks always ask for the recipe. A deliciously different appetizer, it makes even a plain plate of crackers seem festive.

- 1 package (8 ounces) cream cheese, softened
- 1/4 cup shredded Colby-Monterey Jack cheese
- 3 to 4 tablespoons minced fresh cilantro
- 2 to 3 tablespoons grated onion
- 1 tablespoon chili powder
- 1 teaspoon dried minced garlic
- 1/2 teaspoon garlic salt
- 1/4 teaspoon dried oregano
- 1/4 teaspoon crushed red pepper flakes
- 1/8 teaspoon ground cumin
- 1/8 to 1/4 teaspoon hot pepper sauce
- 1/4 cup minced fresh parsley
  Assorted crackers

In a mixing bowl, beat cream cheese. Add the next 10 ingredients and mix well. Cover and refrigerate for at least 1 hour. Shape into a ball. Roll in parsley. Cover and refrigerate for 8 hours or overnight. Serve with crackers. Refrigerate leftovers. **Yield:** 1 cheese ball.

Ricotta Pepperoni Dip

(Pictured below)

Barbara Carlucci, Orange Park, Florida

This warm appetizer dip gets its flavor from an herb soup mix. Crispy golden pizza dough strips are perfect for digging into the thick cheesy mixture.

PIZZA STICKS:
- 1 tube (10 ounces) refrigerated pizza crust
- 1 tablespoon olive oil
- 2 tablespoons grated Parmesan cheese
- 1 tablespoon Italian seasoning
- 1/4 teaspoon garlic powder
- 1/8 teaspoon pepper

DIP:
- 1 cup (8 ounces) sour cream
- 1 cup ricotta cheese
- 1 tablespoon savory herb with garlic soup mix
- 1/4 cup chopped pepperoni
- 1 cup (4 ounces) shredded mozzarella cheese
- 1 tablespoon grated Parmesan cheese

On a lightly floured surface, roll out pizza crust to a 12-in. x 8-in. rectangle. Brush with oil. Combine the Parmesan cheese, Italian seasoning, garlic powder and pepper; sprinkle over dough. Cut into 3-in. x 1-in. strips; place on a greased baking sheet. Bake at 425° for 6-9 minutes or until golden brown.

Meanwhile, combine the sour cream, ricotta, soup mix and pepperoni in a saucepan; heat through. Stir in mozzarella and Parmesan cheeses just until melted. Serve warm with pizza sticks. **Yield:** about 2-1/2 dozen pizza sticks and 2 cups dip.

Hot Mushroom Dip

(Pictured above)

Ellen Derflinger, Jefferson, Maryland

I've whipped up this dip for many potlucks and special gatherings, and it's always well received. Serve this thick hearty spread with crackers, or let it bring new life to a veggie tray.

    4 bacon strips, diced
 1/2 pound fresh mushrooms, chopped
    1 medium onion, finely chopped
    1 garlic clove, minced
    2 tablespoons all-purpose flour
 1/4 teaspoon salt
 1/8 teaspoon pepper
    1 package (8 ounces) cream cheese, cubed
 1/2 cup sour cream
    2 teaspoons Worcestershire sauce
    1 teaspoon soy sauce
Assorted raw vegetables *or* crackers

In a skillet, cook bacon over medium heat until crisp. Remove bacon to paper towels. Drain, reserving 2 tablespoons drippings. In the drippings, saute mushrooms, onion and garlic until tender. Add the flour, salt and pepper; cook and stir for 1 minute or until thickened.

Reduce heat. Add the cream cheese, sour cream, Worcestershire sauce and soy sauce; cook and stir until cheese is melted. Stir in bacon. Serve warm with vegetables or crackers. Refrigerate leftovers. **Yield:** 2 cups.

Peanut Butter Dip

Kristen Proulx, Canton, New York

Both children and adults love this dip, which includes mini chocolate chips. It's so easy to whip up.

 1/2 cup vanilla yogurt
 1/2 cup peanut butter

 1/4 teaspoon ground cinnamon
 1/4 cup miniature semisweet chocolate chips
Apple wedges and miniature pretzels

In a small bowl, combine the yogurt, peanut butter and cinnamon. Stir in chocolate chips. Serve with apples and pretzels. **Yield:** 1 cup.

Double Chili Cheese Dip

(Pictured below)

Linda Keller, Sylvania, Ohio

This rich and zesty dip for tortilla chips can be made in a jiffy when the munchies strike. My husband and I often have it as a late-night snack after the kids are all in bed.

 Uses less fat, sugar or salt. Includes Nutritional Analysis and Diabetic Exchanges.

    1 package (8 ounces) reduced-fat cream cheese, softened
    1 can (15 ounces) turkey chili without beans
    4 green onions, thinly sliced
    3 tablespoons chopped green chilies
 1/4 cup sliced ripe olives, optional
    1 cup (4 ounces) shredded reduced-fat cheddar cheese
Baked tortilla chips

Spread cream cheese into a 9-in. pie plate or quiche dish that has been coated with nonstick cooking spray. Top with chili, onions, chilies and olives if desired. Sprinkle with cheese. Bake, uncovered, at 350° for 15-20 minutes or until the cheese is melted. Serve with tortilla chips. Refrigerate leftovers. **Yield:** 8 servings.

Nutritional Analysis: One serving (calculated without olives and tortilla chips) equals 189 calories, 502 mg sodium, 35 mg cholesterol, 5 g carbohydrate, 12 g protein, 14 g fat. **Diabetic Exchanges:** 1-1/2 fat, 1 meat, 1/2 starch.

Hot Kielbasa Dip

(Pictured at right)

Mary Bondegard, Brooksville, Florida

My husband and I are retired, and I like to look for simple, speedy ways to cook. This thick cheesy dip, with the unusual addition of sausage, goes together in a jiffy. Accompanied by crackers or fresh veggies, it's a hearty appetizer for a football party or family gathering.

> 1 package (8 ounces) cream cheese
> 1/2 cup sour cream
> 1/3 cup milk
> 1 tablespoon mayonnaise
> 1/2 teaspoon Worcestershire sauce
> 8 ounces fully cooked kielbasa *or* Polish sausage, finely chopped
> 1/2 cup sliced green onions, *divided*
> 1/4 cup grated Parmesan cheese
> Assorted crackers *or* raw vegetables

In a 1-1/2-qt. microwave-safe bowl, heat cream cheese, uncovered, on high for 1 minute. Stir in the sour cream, milk, mayonnaise and Worcestershire sauce. Add the kielbasa, 1/4 cup of onions and Parmesan cheese; mix well. Microwave, uncovered, on high for 3-4 minutes or until heated through, stirring once. Sprinkle with remaining onions. Serve with crackers or vegetables. Store in the refrigerator. **Yield:** about 3 cups.

Editor's Note: This recipe was tested in an 850-watt microwave.

Dried Beef Dip

Camie Schuiteman, Marion, Indiana

A friend shared this recipe with me many years ago, and it continues to be a hit. Serve it with potato chips, crackers or raw veggies for a snack, or dollop it on baked potatoes at dinnertime.

> 1 package (8 ounces) cream cheese, softened
> 2 cups (16 ounces) sour cream
> 1 carton (16 ounces) French onion dip
> 1 package (2-1/2 ounces) dried beef, chopped
> Ridged potato chips

In a small mixing bowl, beat the cream cheese, sour cream and dip. Stir in the beef. Serve with chips. Refrigerate leftovers. **Yield:** about 5 cups.

Crab Au Gratin Spread

Suzanne Zick, Lincolnton, North Carolina

For a warm and winning appetizer, I serve this special cracker spread. It's rich tasting and easy to whip up with convenient canned crab.

> 2 tablespoons plus 1 teaspoon butter, *divided*
> 3 tablespoons all-purpose flour
> 1/2 teaspoon salt
> 1/8 teaspoon paprika
> 1/2 cup half-and-half cream
> 1/2 cup milk

> 1/4 cup white wine *or* chicken broth
> 1 can (6 ounces) crabmeat, drained, flaked and cartilage removed *or* 2/3 cup chopped imitation crabmeat
> 1 can (4 ounces) mushroom stems and pieces, drained and chopped
> 1-1/2 teaspoons snipped chives
> 1/2 cup shredded cheddar cheese
> 1 tablespoon dry bread crumbs
> Assorted crackers

In a saucepan, melt 2 tablespoons butter. Stir in the flour, salt and paprika until smooth. Gradually add cream, milk and wine or broth. Bring to a boil; cook and stir for 1-2 minutes or until thickened. Stir in the crab, mushrooms and chives; heat through. Stir in cheese just until melted.

Transfer to a greased shallow 1-qt. baking dish. Melt remaining butter; toss with bread crumbs. Sprinkle over crab mixture. Bake, uncovered, at 400° for 10-15 minutes or until bubbly. Let stand for 5 minutes. Serve with crackers. Refrigerate leftovers. **Yield:** about 2 cups.

Parmesan Fondue

Gwynne Fleener, Coeur d'Alene, Idaho

This recipe was given to me many years ago at a New Year's potluck. Since then, it has been a tradition to serve it at our holiday open house. The creamy mixture is always a hit.

> 1-1/2 to 2 cups milk
> 2 packages (8 ounces *each*) cream cheese, cubed
> 1-1/2 cups grated Parmesan cheese
> 1/2 teaspoon garlic salt
> 1 loaf (1 pound) French bread, cubed

In a large saucepan, cook and stir the milk and cream cheese over low heat until cheese is melted. Stir in Parmesan cheese and garlic salt; cook and stir until heated through. Transfer to a fondue pot or mini slow cooker; keep warm. Serve with bread cubes. Refrigerate leftovers. **Yield:** about 3-1/2 cups.

Cheesy Corn Spread

(Pictured at right)

Jan Henderson, Smackover, Arkansas

Canned Mexicorn lends a sweet twist to this cheesy crowd-pleaser.

    1 **can (11 ounces) Mexicorn, drained**
  1/2 **cup sour cream**
  1/2 **cup mayonnaise**
    1 **can (4 ounces) chopped green chilies, undrained**
  1/4 **cup chopped onion**
    1 **jalapeno pepper, seeded and finely chopped***
    1 **tablespoon ground cumin**
    1 **tablespoon picante sauce**
    3 **cups (12 ounces) shredded cheddar cheese**
  1/2 **cup chopped sweet red pepper**
Assorted crackers

In a bowl, combine the first eight ingredients; stir in cheese. Sprinkle with red pepper. Cover; chill for 4 hours. Serve with crackers. Refrigerate leftovers. **Yield:** 4 cups.

    Editor's Note: When cutting or seeding hot peppers, use rubber or plastic gloves to protect your hands. Avoid touching your face.

Almond Curry Spread

Barbara Beard, Lexington, Kentucky

Curry and chutney combine nicely in this out-of-the-ordinary spread. For dippers, use thick apple slices, carrot sticks, crackers, cocktail bread or a combination of these.

    2 **packages (8 ounces *each*) cream cheese,**
      softened
  1/2 **cup chopped green onions**
  1/3 **cup chopped sweet red pepper**
    1 **tablespoon curry powder**

    2 **teaspoons Worcestershire sauce**
    2 **teaspoons Dijon mustard**
    1 **teaspoon ground nutmeg**
    1 **jar (9 ounces) chutney**
  1/2 **cup slivered almonds, toasted**
Assorted fruit, vegetables *or* crackers

In a mixing bowl, beat cream cheese until smooth. Add onions, red pepper, curry powder, Worcestershire sauce, mustard and nutmeg; mix well. Spread onto a platter. Top with chutney; sprinkle with almonds. Serve with fruit, vegetables or crackers. Refrigerate leftovers. **Yield:** 8-10 servings.

Warm Bacon Cheese Spread

(Pictured at left)

Nicole Marcotte, Smithers, British Columbia

My friends threaten not to come by unless this dip is on the menu! The rich spread bakes right in the bread bowl and goes well with almost any dipper. Plus, cleanup is a breeze.

      1 **round loaf (1 pound) sourdough bread**
      1 **package (8 ounces) cream cheese, softened**
1-1/2 **cups (12 ounces) sour cream**
      2 **cups (8 ounces) shredded cheddar cheese**
1-1/2 **teaspoons Worcestershire sauce**
   3/4 **pound sliced bacon, cooked and crumbled**
   1/2 **cup chopped green onions**
Assorted crackers

Cut the top fourth off the loaf of bread; carefully hollow out the bottom, leaving a 1-in. shell. Cut the removed bread and top of loaf into cubes; set aside.

    In a mixing bowl, beat cream cheese. Add sour cream, cheddar cheese and Worcestershire sauce until combined; stir in bacon and onions. Spoon into bread shell. Wrap in a piece of heavy-duty foil (about 24 in. x 17 in.). Bake at 325° for 1 hour or until heated through. Serve with crackers and reserved bread cubes. **Yield:** 4 cups.

Smoked Salmon Cheesecake

(Pictured below)

Becky Applebee, Chiniak, Alaska

We live on Kodiak Island off the coast of Alaska. Salmon is one of our favorite foods. This elegant dish was the star attraction at the open house we hosted at my husband's business.

>   3 tablespoons dry bread crumbs
>   5 tablespoons grated Parmesan cheese, *divided*
>   1/2 cup chopped onion
>   1/2 cup chopped green pepper
>   3 tablespoons butter
>   4 packages (three 8 ounces, one 3 ounces)
>   cream cheese, softened
>   1/2 cup heavy whipping cream
>   1/4 teaspoon pepper
>   4 eggs
>   5 ounces smoked salmon, diced
>   1/2 cup shredded Swiss cheese
> **Assorted crackers**

Grease the bottom and sides of a 9-in. springform pan. Combine the bread crumbs and 2 tablespoons Parmesan cheese; sprinkle into pan, coating bottom and sides. Set aside.

In a skillet, saute onion and green pepper in butter until tender; set aside. In a mixing bowl, beat cream cheese until fluffy. Beat in the cream, pepper and remaining Parmesan cheese. Add eggs; beat on low speed just until combined. Fold in the onion mixture, salmon and Swiss cheese.

Wrap a double thickness of heavy-duty foil around bottom of prepared pan. Pour salmon mixture into pan. Place in a larger baking pan. Fill larger pan with hot water to a depth of 1-1/2 in. Bake at 325° for 35-40 minutes or until center is almost set. Cool on a wire rack for 1 hour. Refrigerate overnight.

Remove foil and sides of pan. Cut cheesecake into wedges; serve with crackers. **Yield:** 12-14 servings.

Creamy Chicken Spread

(Pictured above)

Charlene Barrows, Reedley, California

✓ Uses less fat, sugar or salt. Includes Nutritional Analysis and Diabetic Exchanges.

Every time I take this eye-catching log to a party, it's gone in no time. This mild spread smooths easily onto any kind of cracker.

>   1 package (8 ounces) cream cheese, softened
>   1/4 cup mayonnaise
>   2 tablespoons lemon juice
>   1/2 teaspoon salt
>   1/4 teaspoon ground ginger
>   1/8 teaspoon pepper
>   1/8 teaspoon hot pepper sauce
>   2 cups finely chopped cooked chicken breast
>   2 hard-cooked eggs, finely chopped
>   1/4 cup sliced green onions
> **Diced pimientos and additional sliced green onions**
> **Assorted crackers and snack bread**

In a small mixing bowl, combine the first seven ingredients; mix well. Stir in chicken, eggs and green onions. Shape into an 8-in. x 2-in. log. Garnish with pimientos and onions. Cover and chill. Remove from the refrigerator 15 minutes before serving. Serve with crackers and snack bread. Refrigerate leftovers. **Yield:** 3 cups.

Nutritional Analysis: 1/4 cup of spread (prepared with reduced-fat cream cheese and fat-free mayonnaise) equals 100 calories, 5 g fat (3 g saturated fat), 67 mg cholesterol, 223 mg sodium, 3 g carbohydrate, trace fiber, 10 g protein. **Diabetic Exchanges:** 1 lean meat, 1 fat.

RYE PARTY PUFFS

NO-YOLK DEVILED EGGS

VEGGIE PARTY PIZZA

MARINATED SHRIMP

FRUIT 'N' CHEESE KABOBS

CUCUMBER CANAPES

COLD APPETIZERS

Appetizer Roll-Ups

Marcella Funk, Salem, Oregon

Cream cheese, herbs and vegetables make even deli cold cuts a fancy and filling appetizer. Bite-size pieces look so pretty set on a serving platter in a circle. The arrangement never stays complete for long once this snack is served.

ROAST BEEF:
  4 ounces cream cheese, softened
  1/4 cup minced fresh cilantro
  2 to 3 tablespoons minced banana peppers*
  1 garlic clove, minced
  1/2 pound thinly sliced cooked roast beef
HAM AND TURKEY:
  12 ounces cream cheese, softened
  1/2 cup shredded carrot
  1/2 cup shredded zucchini
  4 teaspoons dill weed
  1/2 pound thinly sliced fully cooked ham
  1/2 pound thinly sliced cooked turkey

In a bowl, combine the cream cheese, cilantro, peppers and garlic. Spread about 2 tablespoons on each slice of beef. Roll up tightly and wrap in plastic wrap.

In another bowl, combine cream cheese, carrot, zucchini and dill. Spread about 2 tablespoons on each slice of ham and turkey. Roll up tightly; wrap in plastic wrap. Refrigerate overnight. Slice into 1-1/2-in. pieces. **Yield:** 6-7 dozen.

*Editor's Note: When cutting or seeding hot peppers, use rubber or plastic gloves to protect your hands. Avoid touching your face.

Veggie Party Pizza

(Pictured above)

Laura Kadlec, Maiden Rock, Wisconsin

I originally made this yummy veggie pizza to share with a friend who was watching her cholesterol.

✓ Uses less fat, sugar or salt. Includes Nutritional Analysis and Diabetic Exchanges.

  2 cups all-purpose flour
  2 teaspoons baking powder
  1 teaspoon salt
  2/3 cup fat-free milk
  1/4 cup plus 1 tablespoon canola oil, *divided*
TOPPING:
  3 cups 2% cottage cheese
  1 envelope ranch salad dressing mix
  1/2 cup fat-free mayonnaise
  1/4 cup fat-free milk
  1-1/2 cups chopped broccoli
  1-1/2 cups chopped cauliflower
  1/2 cup chopped celery
  1/3 cup shredded carrot
  1/4 cup chopped onion
  2 cups (8 ounces) shredded part-skim
    mozzarella cheese
Sliced ripe *or* stuffed olives, optional

For crust, combine flour, baking powder and salt. Add milk and 1/4 cup oil; mix well. Shape into a ball; knead 10 times. Press onto the bottom and up the sides of an ungreased 15-in. x 10-in. x 1-in. baking pan. Prick with a fork; brush with remaining oil. Bake at 425° for 12-14 minutes or until edges are lightly browned. Cool.

In a mixing bowl, combine cottage cheese, ranch dressing mix, mayonnaise and milk; spread over crust. Sprinkle with vegetables and cheese. Garnish with olives if desired. Refrigerate until serving. **Yield:** 14 servings.

Nutritional Analysis: One serving (calculated without olives) equals 234 calories, 11 g fat (3 g saturated fat), 15 mg cholesterol, 592 mg sodium, 21 g carbohydrate, 1 g fiber, 14 g protein. **Diabetic Exchanges:** 2 vegetable, 1 starch, 1 lean meat, 1 fat.

Oriental Pork Tenderloin

Diana Beyer, Graham, Washington

I first made this appetizer on Christmas Eve a few years ago, and it has since become a tradition. Serve the pork slices alone or on small dinner rolls with hot mustard sauce, ketchup or horseradish.

  1 cup soy sauce
  1/2 cup packed brown sugar
  2 tablespoons red wine vinegar
  2 teaspoons red food coloring, optional
  1 garlic clove, minced
  1 teaspoon ground ginger
  1 teaspoon salt
  1/2 teaspoon pepper
  3 pork tenderloins (about 1 pound *each*)
Sesame seeds, toasted

In a bowl, combine the first eight ingredients; mix well. Remove 1/2 cup for basting; cover and refrigerate. Pour the remaining marinade into a large resealable plastic bag; add tenderloins. Seal bag and turn to coat; refrigerate overnight.

Drain and discard marinade. Place the pork on a rack in a shallow roasting pan. Bake, uncovered, at 350° for 55-60 minutes or until a meat thermometer reads 160°, brushing with reserved marinade every 15 minutes. Sprinkle with sesame seeds. Cool for 30 minutes. Refrigerate for 2 hours or overnight. Cut into thin slices. **Yield:** 8-10 servings.

Rye Party Puffs

(Pictured below)

Kelly Thornberry, La Porte, Indiana

I can't go anywhere without taking along my puffs. They're pretty enough for a wedding reception yet hearty enough to snack on while watching football on television. A platterful of these will vanish even with a small group.

        1 cup water
    1/2 cup butter
    1/2 cup all-purpose flour
    1/2 cup rye flour
        2 teaspoons dried parsley flakes
    1/2 teaspoon garlic powder
    1/4 teaspoon salt
        4 eggs
    Caraway seeds
    CORNED BEEF FILLING:
        2 packages (8 ounces *each*) cream cheese, softened
        2 packages (2-1/2 ounces *each*) thinly sliced cooked corned beef, chopped
    1/2 cup mayonnaise
    1/4 cup sour cream
        2 tablespoons minced chives
        2 tablespoons diced onion
        1 teaspoon spicy brown *or* horseradish mustard
    1/8 teaspoon garlic powder
       10 small stuffed olives, chopped

In a saucepan over medium heat, bring water and butter to a boil. Add flours, parsley, garlic powder and salt all at once; stir until a smooth ball forms. Remove from the heat; let stand for 5 minutes. Beat in eggs, one at time. Beat until smooth.

Drop batter by rounded teaspoonfuls 2 in. apart onto greased baking sheets. Sprinkle with caraway. Bake at 400° for 18-20 minutes or until golden. Remove to wire racks. Immediately cut a slit in each puff to allow steam to escape; cool. In a mixing bowl, combine the first eight filling ingredients; mix well. Stir in olives. Split puffs; add filling. Refrigerate until serving. **Yield:** 4-1/2 dozen.

Asparagus Beef Roll-Ups

Linda Senuta, Gettysburg, Pennsylvania

I first sampled this hearty appetizer at a dinner party. These roll-ups were the first thing to disappear from the table.

        2 tablespoons heavy whipping cream
        2 tablespoons sour cream
        2 to 4 teaspoons prepared horseradish
    1/4 teaspoon grated lemon peel
    1/4 teaspoon salt
    Dash pepper
        4 flour tortillas (7 inches)
        4 thin slices cooked roast beef
        4 fresh asparagus spears, cooked and drained

In a small mixing bowl, beat whipping cream until soft peaks form. Fold in sour cream, horseradish, lemon peel, salt and pepper. Spread about 2 teaspoons on each tortilla; top with a slice of beef. Spread with the remaining cream mixture. Place an asparagus spear at one end; roll up tightly. Wrap in plastic wrap. Refrigerate for at least 2 hours. Cut into 1/2-in. slices. **Yield:** about 4 dozen.

Tangy Mozzarella Bites

Julie Wasem, Aurora, Nebraska

I adapted this recipe from one I found years ago, substituting ingredients most people have on hand. I like to serve it with crackers or small bread slices.

    1/4 cup olive oil
        1 to 2 teaspoons balsamic vinegar
        1 garlic clove, minced
        1 teaspoon dried basil
        1 teaspoon coarsely ground pepper
        1 pound mozzarella cheese, cut into 1/2-inch cubes

In a bowl, combine the oil, vinegar, garlic, basil and pepper. Add cheese; toss to coat. Cover and refrigerate for at least 1 hour. **Yield:** about 3 cups.

1 medium tomato, chopped
3/4 cup shredded cheddar cheese
3/4 cup shredded mozzarella cheese
1 cup shredded lettuce

Unroll the crescent roll dough and place in an ungreased 15-in. x 10-in. x 1-in. baking pan. Flatten dough to fit the pan, sealing seams and perforations. Bake at 375° for 8-10 minutes or until crust is light golden brown; cool. In a small bowl, blend the cream cheese and sour cream with a wire whisk; spread over the crust. Chill for 30 minutes.

Meanwhile, in a skillet, cook beef over medium heat until no longer pink; drain. Stir in taco seasoning. Add water according to package directions and simmer for 5 minutes, stirring occasionally. Spread over cream cheese layer. Top with olives, tomato, cheeses and lettuce. Cut into serving-size pieces. Refrigerate until serving. **Yield:** 12-16 servings.

Pretty Ham Pinwheels

Plan ahead to slice party-perfect appetizers from these zippy rolls. They're easy to assemble and sure to be a hit when you present a pretty plateful at any gathering. Our Test Kitchen home economists came up with the recipe.

1 package (3 ounces) cream cheese, softened
1 garlic clove, minced
1/4 teaspoon curry powder
1/4 teaspoon ground mustard
1 cup shredded peeled tart apple
4 flour tortillas (7 inches)
1/4 cup chopped sweet red pepper
2 green onions, thinly sliced
4 thin slices fully cooked ham

In a mixing bowl, beat the cream cheese, garlic, curry powder and mustard. Stir in apple. Spread about 2 tablespoons over each tortilla. Layer with the red pepper, onions and ham. Roll up tightly and wrap in plastic wrap. Refrigerate for at least 2 hours. Cut into 1-in. slices. **Yield:** about 2 dozen.

Marinated Mushrooms

JoAnn Stevens, Durham, North Carolina

These are a nice addition to an appetizer buffet table. For the best flavor, allow the mushrooms to marinate a few days before serving.

1 pound fresh whole mushrooms
1 large onion, sliced
3/4 cup olive oil
1/4 cup white vinegar
2 garlic cloves, minced
1/2 teaspoon salt
1/4 teaspoon ground mustard
1/8 teaspoon pepper
Crushed red pepper flakes to taste

In a large bowl, combine all ingredients. Cover and refrigerate for 1 to 2 days. Serve with a slotted spoon. **Yield:** 6-8 servings.

Cheese-Stuffed Cherry Tomatoes

(Pictured above)

Mary Lou Robison, Miami, Florida

We live close to some of the best tomato fields. I use the miniature variety for this recipe. They're delicious.

1 pint cherry tomatoes
4 ounces crumbled feta cheese
1/2 cup finely chopped red onion
1/2 cup olive oil
1/4 cup red wine vinegar
1 tablespoon dried oregano
Salt and pepper to taste

Cut a thin slice off the top of each tomato. Scoop out and discard pulp. Invert tomatoes onto paper towels to drain. Combine cheese and onion; spoon into tomatoes.

In a jar with a tight-fitting lid, combine oil, vinegar, oregano, salt and pepper; shake well. Spoon over tomatoes. Cover and refrigerate for 30 minutes or until serving. **Yield:** about 1 dozen.

Mexican Pizza

Sandra McKenzie, Braham, Minnesota

My husband and I created the recipe for this hearty snack. Our whole family enjoys it.

2 tubes (8 ounces *each*) refrigerated crescent rolls
1 package (8 ounces) cream cheese, softened
1 cup (8 ounces) sour cream
1 pound ground beef
1 envelope taco seasoning mix
1 can (2-1/4 ounces) sliced ripe olives, drained

Cucumber Shrimp Appetizers

Patricia Kile, Greentown, Pennsylvania

When my friend's husband needed lower-fat snacks, she served him this fresh-tasting shrimp spread. Cucumber slices are a fun and healthy alternative to crackers.

✓ Uses less fat, sugar or salt. Includes Nutritional Analysis and Diabetic Exchanges.

  1 can (8 ounces) unsweetened crushed
     pineapple, drained
  1 can (4 ounces) tiny shrimp, rinsed and drained
1/4 cup reduced-fat mayonnaise
  1 tablespoon finely chopped green onion
  2 teaspoons Dijon mustard
1-1/2 teaspoons minced fresh dill
  1 medium cucumber (8 inches), cut into 1/4-inch
     slices
Fresh dill sprigs, optional

In a bowl, combine pineapple, shrimp, mayonnaise, onion, mustard and dill. Spoon onto cucumber slices. Garnish with dill sprigs if desired. **Yield:** 32 appetizers.

    Nutritional Analysis: One appetizer equals 16 calories, 1 g fat (trace saturated fat), 7 mg cholesterol, 29 mg sodium, 2 g carbohydrate, trace fiber, 1 g protein. **Diabetic Exchange:** Free food.

Christmas Party Pinwheels

(Pictured below)

Janis Plourde, Smooth Rock Falls, Ontario

These festive appetizers look so special and pretty that folks can't resist them! The refreshing flavor of ranch dressing and crisp colorful vegetables make these pinwheels a pleasure to serve to holiday guests.

  2 packages (8 ounces *each*) cream cheese, softened
  1 envelope ranch salad dressing mix
1/2 cup minced sweet red pepper
1/2 cup minced celery
1/4 cup sliced green onions
1/4 cup sliced stuffed olives
  3 to 4 flour tortillas (10 inches)

In a mixing bowl, beat cream cheese and dressing mix until smooth. Add red pepper, celery, onions and olives; mix well. Spread about 3/4 cup on each tortilla. Roll up tightly; wrap in plastic wrap. Refrigerate for at least 2 hours. Slice into 1/2-in. pieces. **Yield:** 15-20 servings.

No-Yolk Deviled Eggs

(Pictured above)

Dottie Burton, Cincinnati, Ohio

This lighter recipe still provides traditional deviled egg flavor and appearance. A mashed-potato mixture replaces the traditional yolk filling.

✓ Uses less fat, sugar or salt. Includes Nutritional Analysis and Diabetic Exchanges.

10 hard-cooked eggs
3/4 cup mashed potatoes (prepared with fat-free
    milk and margarine)
  1 tablespoon fat-free mayonnaise
  1 teaspoon prepared mustard
  2 to 3 drops yellow food coloring, optional
Paprika

Slice eggs in half lengthwise; remove yolks and refrigerate for another use. Set whites aside. In a small bowl, combine mashed potatoes, mayonnaise, mustard and food coloring if desired; mix well. Stuff or pipe into egg whites. Sprinkle with paprika. Refrigerate until serving. **Yield:** 10 servings.

    Nutritional Analysis: One serving equals 35 calories, 118 mg sodium, trace cholesterol, 3 g carbohydrate, 4 g protein, 1 g fat. **Diabetic Exchanges:** 1/2 very lean meat, 1/2 vegetable.

Eggscellent Idea

Deviled eggs will be more stable, and sit flat without wobbling, if you cut off a tiny piece from the bottom of each half.

Spinach Deviled Eggs

Dorothy Sander, Evansville, Indiana

Spinach adds unexpected color and flavor to this tasty variation on deviled eggs. They're easy to make with leftover Easter eggs…and an attractive addition to a party spread.

    12 hard-cooked eggs
    1/4 cup mayonnaise
     2 tablespoons vinegar
     2 tablespoons butter, softened
     1 tablespoon sugar
    1/2 teaspoon pepper
    1/4 teaspoon salt
    1/2 cup frozen chopped spinach, thawed and
        squeezed dry
     4 bacon strips, cooked and crumbled

Slice eggs in half lengthwise; remove yolks and set whites aside. In a small bowl, mash yolks with a fork. Stir in the mayonnaise, vinegar, butter, sugar, pepper and salt. Add spinach and mix well. Stir in the bacon; spoon into egg whites. Serve immediately. **Yield:** 2 dozen.

Fruit 'n' Cheese Kabobs

(Pictured below)

The home economists in our Test Kitchen came up with this colorful combination. It's a simple, nutritious snack that's a snap to put together.

    1 block (1 pound) Colby-Monterey Jack cheese
    1 block (1 pound) cheddar cheese
    1 block (1 pound) baby Swiss cheese
    1 fresh pineapple, peeled, cored and cut
        into 2-inch chunks
    1 to 2 pounds seedless green *or* red grapes
    3 pints strawberries

Cut cheese into chunks or slices. If desired, cut into shapes with small cutters. Alternately thread cheese and fruit onto wooden skewers. Serve immediately. **Yield:** about 3 dozen.

Colorful Crab Appetizer Pizza

Diane Caron, Des Moines, Iowa

If you're looking for a really easy and special appetizer, this one stands out. It's a fresh-tasting and lovely variation on a cold vegetable pizza. I make it as a snack for parties all the time and even for a light main dish served along with a soup or salad.

     1 tube (8 ounces) refrigerated crescent rolls
     1 package (8 ounces) cream cheese, softened
    1-1/2 cups coarsely chopped fresh spinach,
        divided
     1 green onion, thinly sliced
    1-1/2 teaspoons minced fresh dill *or* 1/2 teaspoon
        dill weed
     1 teaspoon grated lemon peel, *divided*
    1/2 teaspoon lemon juice
    1/8 teaspoon pepper
    1-1/4 cups chopped imitation crabmeat
    1/4 cup chopped ripe olives

Unroll crescent roll dough and place on an ungreased 12-in. pizza pan. Flatten dough, sealing seams and perforations. Bake at 350° for 8-10 minutes or until lightly browned; cool.

In a small mixing bowl, beat cream cheese until smooth. Stir in 1 cup spinach, onion, dill, 1/2 teaspoon lemon peel, lemon juice and pepper. Spread over the crust. Top with crab, olives and remaining spinach and lemon peel. Cut into bite-size squares. Refrigerate until serving. **Yield:** 8-10 servings.

Ham Roll-Ups

Kathleen Green, Republic, Missouri

Green onions and ripe olives give lively flavor and color to these bite-size appetizers. Calling for just four simple ingredients, they're quick to assemble and can be made the day before they're needed. They're very popular with my friends and family no matter how many times I serve them at gatherings.

✓ **Uses less fat, sugar or salt. Includes Nutritional Analysis and Diabetic Exchanges.**

    1 package (8 ounces) cream cheese, softened
    1 can (2-1/4 ounces) chopped ripe olives,
        drained
    1/3 cup thinly sliced green onions
    8 to 10 thin slices fully cooked ham

In a mixing bowl, beat cream cheese until smooth; stir in the olives and onions. Spread over ham slices. Roll up, jelly-roll style, starting with a short side. Chill for at least 1 hour. Just before serving, cut into 1-in. pieces. **Yield:** 40 appetizers.

Nutritional Analysis: One serving of 2 roll-ups (prepared with fat-free cream cheese and reduced-fat ham) equals 27 calories, 259 mg sodium, 7 mg cholesterol, 1 g carbohydrate, 4 g protein, 1 g fat. **Diabetic Exchange:** 1/2 meat.

Antipasto Platter

(Pictured above)

Teri Lindquist, Gurnee, Illinois

We entertain often, and this is one of our favorite party pleasers. It's such a refreshing change from the usual chips and dip.

      1 jar (24 ounces) pepperoncinis, drained
      1 can (15 ounces) garbanzo beans *or* chickpeas,
         rinsed and drained
      2 cups halved fresh mushrooms
      2 cups halved cherry tomatoes
    1/2 pound provolone cheese, cubed
      1 can (6 ounces) pitted ripe olives, drained
      1 package (3-1/2 ounces) sliced pepperoni
      1 bottle (8 ounces) Italian vinaigrette dressing
Lettuce leaves

In a large bowl, combine peppers, beans, mushrooms, tomatoes, cheese, olives and pepperoni. Pour vinaigrette over mixture; gently toss to coat. Refrigerate for at least 30 minutes or overnight. Arrange on a lettuce-lined platter. Serve with toothpicks. **Yield:** 14-16 servings.

Chicken Salad Puffs

Lola Pullen, Lakeland, Florida

Stuffed with chicken salad, these pretty golden puffs are perfect for a buffet. Folks seem to enjoy the subtle sweetness from the pineapple and the crunch of the celery and pecans.

      1 cup water
    1/2 cup butter
    1/2 teaspoon salt
      1 cup all-purpose flour
      4 eggs
FILLING:
      2 cups finely chopped cooked chicken
      1 can (8 ounces) crushed pineapple, drained
    1/2 cup mayonnaise
    1/4 cup chopped celery
    1/4 cup thinly sliced green onions
    1/4 cup chopped pecans
      2 tablespoons sweet pickle relish
    1/4 teaspoon onion salt
    1/4 teaspoon garlic salt
    1/4 teaspoon paprika
Salt and pepper to taste

In a saucepan, bring water, butter and salt to a boil. Add flour all at once and stir until a smooth ball forms. Remove from the heat; let stand for 5 minutes. Add eggs, one at a time, beating well after each addition. Continue beating until smooth and shiny.

Drop by rounded teaspoonfuls 2 in. apart onto a greased baking sheet. Bake at 400° for 15-20 minutes or until golden brown. Remove to wire racks. Immediately cut a slit in each puff to allow steam to escape; cool. Split puffs and set tops aside; remove soft dough from inside.

In a bowl, combine all of the filling ingredients and mix well. Fill the puffs and replace the tops. Refrigerate until serving. Refrigerate any leftovers. **Yield:** about 3-1/2 dozen.

Cucumber Canapes

(Pictured below)

Nadine Whittaker, South Plymouth, Massachusetts

I always get requests for the recipe whenever I serve these delicate finger sandwiches with a creamy herb spread and festive red and green garnishes.

- 1 cup mayonnaise
- 1 package (3 ounces) cream cheese, softened
- 1 tablespoon grated onion
- 1 tablespoon minced chives
- 1/2 teaspoon cider vinegar
- 1/2 teaspoon Worcestershire sauce
- 1 garlic clove, minced
- 1/4 teaspoon paprika
- 1/8 teaspoon curry powder
- 1/8 teaspoon *each* dried oregano, thyme, basil, parsley flakes and dill weed
- 1 loaf (1 pound) white *or* rye bread
- 2 medium cucumbers, scored and thinly sliced

Diced pimientos and additional dill weed

In a blender or food processor, combine the mayonnaise, cream cheese, onion, chives, vinegar, Worcestershire sauce and seasonings. Cover and process until blended. Cover and refrigerate for 24 hours.

Using a 2-1/2-in. biscuit cutter, cut out circles from bread slices. Spread mayonnaise mixture over bread; top with cucumber slices. Garnish with pimientos and dill. **Yield:** 2 dozen.

Veggie Tortilla Pinwheels

Doris Ann Yoder, Arthur, Illinois

These bite-size snacks are delicious any time of the day. Simply combine cream cheese, dried beef, chopped vegetables and salad dressing mix, then roll into tortillas, refrigerate, slice and serve.

- 1 package (8 ounces) cream cheese, softened
- 4 teaspoons ranch salad dressing mix
- 1 package (2-1/4 ounces) dried beef, chopped
- 1/2 cup chopped broccoli
- 1/2 cup chopped cauliflower
- 1/4 cup chopped green onions
- 1/4 cup chopped stuffed olives
- 5 flour tortillas (8 inches)

Salsa, optional

In a mixing bowl, combine the cream cheese and salad dressing mix. Stir in the beef, broccoli, cauliflower, onions and olives. Spread over tortillas; roll up tightly and wrap in plastic wrap. Refrigerate for at least 2 hours. Unwrap and cut into 1/2-in. slices. Serve with salsa if desired. **Yield:** about 5 dozen.

Shrimp-Stuffed Celery

Shirley Watanabe, Kula, Hawaii

The creamy shrimp filling in the crunchy celery sections has a tasty blend of flavors.

- 1 bunch celery, separated into ribs
- 1 package (3 ounces) cream cheese, softened
- 2 tablespoons mayonnaise
- 1 can (6 ounces) tiny shrimp, rinsed and finely chopped
- 1 tablespoon *each* finely chopped onion, green pepper and stuffed olives
- 1 tablespoon minced fresh parsley
- 1 to 2 drops hot pepper sauce
- 1/4 teaspoon salt
- 1/8 teaspoon pepper
- 1/8 teaspoon Worcestershire sauce

Cut celery ribs into 2-in. pieces. Finely chop one piece; set aside. In a mixing bowl, beat cream cheese and mayonnaise until smooth. Stir in the remaining ingredients and reserved chopped celery. Stuff into celery ribs. Refrigerate until serving. **Yield:** about 3 dozen.

Garlic-Mushroom Appetizer

(Pictured above)

Rosanna Houlton, Fort Collins, Colorado

My grandfather, who was a hotel chef for many years, created this recipe. He prepared these mushrooms for big family gatherings, and they always were gone quickly.

    1 cup chopped onion
  1/2 cup olive oil
    3 tablespoons butter
    2 pounds fresh mushrooms, sliced
    1 can (28 ounces) crushed tomatoes in puree,
      undrained
    1 teaspoon salt
  1/4 teaspoon pepper
  1/2 cup red wine vinegar
    1 bunch fresh parsley, finely chopped
      (about 1-1/2 cups)
    3 garlic cloves, minced
Sliced French bread

In a saucepan, saute onion in oil and butter until transparent. Add the mushrooms; cook for 2 minutes. Add tomatoes, salt and pepper; cover and simmer for 20-30 minutes. Add vinegar, parsley and garlic; mix well. Cover and simmer for 10 minutes. Chill several hours or overnight. To serve, spoon onto slices of French bread. **Yield:** 12-16 servings.

Cold Vegetable Pizza

Marlene Reichart, Leesport, Pennsylvania

Even youngsters love this pizza. I've made it for a light lunch and served it as an hors d'oeuvre at a get-together.

    2 tubes (8 ounces *each*) refrigerated crescent rolls
    1 cup mayonnaise
    1 package (8 ounces) cream cheese, softened
    1 tablespoon dill weed
2-1/2 cups mixed chopped fresh vegetables
      (cucumber, radishes, broccoli, onion, green
      pepper, carrots, celery, mushrooms)

  1/2 cup sliced ripe olives
  3/4 cup shredded cheddar cheese
  3/4 cup shredded mozzarella cheese

Unroll the crescent rolls and place in an ungreased 15-in. x 10-in. x 1-in. baking pan. Flatten dough to fit the pan, sealing seams and perforations. Bake at 375° for 10 minutes or until golden brown. Cool.

In a small mixing bowl, beat the mayonnaise, cream cheese and dill until smooth; spread over crust. Top with the vegetables of your choice. Sprinkle with olives and cheeses; press lightly. Cover and chill for at least 1 hour. Cut into squares. **Yield:** 12-15 servings.

Marinated Shrimp

(Pictured below)

Margaret DeLong, Gainesville, Florida

Seafood is a staple here in Florida. This recipe is quick and easy to make and can be prepared well in advance. I always seem to get a lot of requests for the recipe when I make it for a party or special occasion.

    2 pounds cooked medium shrimp, peeled
      and deveined
    1 medium red onion, cut into rings
    2 medium lemons, cut into slices
    1 cup pitted ripe olives
  1/2 cup olive oil
  1/3 cup minced fresh parsley
    3 tablespoons red wine vinegar
    3 tablespoons lemon juice
    1 garlic clove, minced
    1 bay leaf
    1 tablespoon minced fresh basil *or* 1 teaspoon
      dried basil
    1 teaspoon salt
    1 teaspoon ground mustard
  1/4 teaspoon pepper

In a 3-qt. glass serving bowl, combine the shrimp, onion, lemons and olives. In a jar with a tight-fitting lid, combine the remaining ingredients; shake well. Pour over shrimp mixture and stir gently to coat. Cover and refrigerate for 24 hours, stirring occasionally. Discard bay leaf before serving. **Yield:** 14 servings.

PEPPER POPPERS

ASPARAGUS HAM SWIRLS

SAVORY PARTY BREAD

ORANGE-PECAN HOT WINGS

BAKED EGG ROLLS

VEGETABLE TORTILLA STACK

HOT APPETIZERS

Garden Focaccia

(Pictured above)

Mary Ann Ludwig, Edwardsville, Illinois

Frozen bread dough is the convenient base for this herb-flavored flat Italian bread. These savory slices are a super appetizer at a summer gathering. It's a fun and delicious way to use up abundant garden tomatoes and fresh zucchini.

✓ Uses less fat, sugar or salt. Includes Nutritional Analysis and Diabetic Exchanges.

    1 loaf (1 pound) frozen bread dough, thawed
    1 tablespoon olive oil
    1 tablespoon minced fresh rosemary *or* 1
        teaspoon dried rosemary, crushed
    1 tablespoon minced fresh thyme *or* 1
        teaspoon dried thyme
    1 package (8 ounces) cream cheese, softened
1/4 cup finely chopped onion
    1 garlic clove, minced
    4 large fresh mushrooms, sliced
    3 medium tomatoes, sliced
    1 small zucchini, thinly sliced
1/4 cup grated Parmesan cheese

On a lightly floured surface, roll dough into a 15-in. x 10-in. rectangle. Place in a greased 15-in. x 10-in. x 1-in. baking pan. Cover and let rise for 30 minutes. Using your fingertips, press indentations into the dough. Brush with oil; sprinkle with rosemary and thyme. Bake at 400° for 12-15 minutes or until golden brown. Cool slightly.

In a mixing bowl, combine cream cheese, onion and garlic. Spread over crust. Top with mushrooms, tomatoes and zucchini; sprinkle with Parmesan cheese. Bake for 12-15 minutes or until lightly browned. Cool for 5 minutes before cutting. **Yield:** 20 slices.

Nutritional Analysis: One slice (prepared with reduced-fat cream cheese) equals 109 calories, 4 g fat (2 g saturated fat), 7 mg cholesterol, 185 mg sodium, 14 g carbohydrate, 1 g fiber, 5 g protein. **Diabetic Exchanges:** 1 vegetable, 1 fat, 1/2 starch.

Tomato Cheese Pinwheels

(Pictured below)

Maggie Gassett, Hillsborough, New Hampshire

These cheesy pinwheels are our favorite for Mother's Day. No matter how many we bake, there are never any left over. The light cheddar tang complements the tomato flavor beautifully. They look complicated but are easy to prepare.

    4 to 4-1/2 cups all-purpose flour, *divided*
    2 tablespoons sugar
    1 package (1/4 ounce) active dry yeast
1-1/4 teaspoons salt
    3/4 cup warm tomato juice (120° to 130°)
    1/2 cup warm water (120° to 130°)
    1/4 cup butter
    1 egg
    2 cups (8 ounces) finely shredded sharp
        cheddar cheese
    2 tablespoons snipped chives

In a mixing bowl, combine 1 cup flour, sugar, yeast and salt. Add tomato juice, water and butter; beat for 2 minutes on medium speed. Add egg and enough remaining flour to form a soft dough. Place in a greased bowl; turn once to grease top. Cover and refrigerate for 2 hours or until doubled.

Punch dough down. Divide in half; roll each half into a 15-in. x 12-in. rectangle approximately 1/8 in. thick. Cut into 3-in. squares. Place 2 in. apart on greased baking sheets. Make 1-in. slits in each corner of each square.

Combine cheese and chives; place 1 heaping teaspoon in the center of each square. Bring every other corner up to center, overlapping slightly to form a pinwheel; press firmly. Bake at 400° for 8-10 minutes. Remove to a wire rack to cool. **Yield:** 40 appetizers.

Spicy Chicken Wings

(Pictured at right)

Varina Caton, Appleton, New York

This area of New York is well known for its chicken wings, and these are the best I've ever tasted. They make great appetizers for all sorts of parties.

- 16 to 18 chicken wings (about 4 pounds)
- Vegetable oil
- 1/2 cup butter, melted
- 1/2 cup hot pepper sauce
- 2 tablespoons cider vinegar
- Carrots and celery sticks
- Blue cheese dressing

Cut the chicken wings into three pieces; discard the wing tips. Heat oil to 375°. Fry chicken in hot oil until crisp and juices run clear (5-7 minutes for the small part, 6-8 minutes for the drumettes).

Combine the butter, hot pepper sauce and vinegar in a bowl; add the chicken and toss to coat. Drain. Serve chicken wings with carrots, celery and dressing. **Yield:** about 3 dozen.

Tangy Onion Flowers

Karen Owen, Rising Sun, Indiana

These flavorful baked onions are a great accompaniment to grilled meat. They aren't crisp like the deep-fried "blooming onions" served in restaurants, but we think they are equally delicious.

✓ Uses less fat, sugar or salt. Includes Nutritional Analysis and Diabetic Exchanges.

- 4 large sweet onions, peeled
- 1/4 cup red wine vinegar
- 1 tablespoon brown sugar
- 1 teaspoon dried oregano
- 1/2 teaspoon salt
- 1/4 teaspoon pepper
- 1/2 cup coarsely crushed fat-free salad croutons

Place the onions root end up on a microwave-safe plate. Microwave, uncovered, on high for 10-12 minutes or until crisp-tender. Invert onto a cutting board. Slice each onion into eight wedges to within 1/2 in. of bottom; fan out. Place each onion on a 12-in. square piece of foil coated with nonstick cooking spray.

In a small bowl, combine vinegar, brown sugar, oregano, salt and pepper. Brush some over onions; set remaining mixture aside. Fold foil around onions; seal tightly. Place on a baking sheet. Bake at 425° for 30-35 minutes or until tender. Open foil carefully. Place onions on a serving platter. Drizzle with remaining vinegar mixture; sprinkle with croutons. **Yield:** 4 onions (8 servings).

Nutritional Analysis: One serving (half of an onion) equals 48 calories, trace fat (trace saturated fat), 0 cholesterol, 203 mg sodium, 11 g carbohydrate, 1 g fiber, 1 g protein. **Diabetic Exchange:** 2 vegetable.

Editor's Note: This recipe was tested in an 850-watt microwave.

Sausage Quiche Squares

Linda Wheeler, Middleburg, Florida

Having done some catering, I especially appreciate interesting, appetizing finger foods. I'm constantly asked to make these popular squares to serve at parties.

- 1 pound bulk pork sausage
- 1 cup (4 ounces) shredded cheddar cheese
- 1 cup (4 ounces) shredded Monterey Jack cheese
- 1/2 cup finely chopped onion
- 1 can (4 ounces) chopped green chilies
- 1 tablespoon minced jalapeno pepper,* optional
- 10 eggs
- 1 teaspoon chili powder
- 1 teaspoon ground cumin
- 1 teaspoon salt
- 1/2 teaspoon garlic powder
- 1/2 teaspoon pepper

In a large skillet, cook sausage until no longer pink; drain. Place in a greased 13-in. x 9-in. x 2-in. baking dish. Layer with cheeses, onion, chilies and jalapeno if desired. In a bowl, beat eggs and seasonings. Pour over cheese. Bake, uncovered, at 375° for 18-22 minutes or until a knife inserted near the center comes out clean. Cool for 10 minutes; cut into 1-in. squares. **Yield:** about 8 dozen.

*Editor's Note: When cutting or seeding hot peppers, use rubber or plastic gloves to protect your hands. Avoid touching your face.

Picking Out Onions

When buying onions, choose those that are heavy for their size with dry, papery skins.

Vegetable Tortilla Stack

(Pictured above)

Irene Muller, Wray, Colorado

These tasty layered tortillas are a hit with my grandchildren. Nutritious vegetables are deliciously disguised in this snack.

  3/4 cup chopped green pepper
  3/4 cup chopped sweet red pepper
   1 small onion, chopped
   2 tablespoons vegetable oil
  1/2 cup picante sauce
   1 package (16 ounces) frozen broccoli-cauliflower
       blend
   6 flour tortillas (8 inches)
   1 can (16 ounces) refried beans
   2 cups (8 ounces) shredded Monterey Jack cheese
   2 cups (8 ounces) shredded cheddar cheese
Minced fresh cilantro, sliced ripe olives, sour cream and
    additional picante sauce

In a skillet, saute peppers and onion in oil until tender. Stir in picante sauce; set aside. Cook frozen vegetables according to package directions; drain. Cool slightly; coarsely chop vegetables.

Place two tortillas on an ungreased baking sheet. Spread each with 1/3 cup refried beans and sprinkle with 1/3 cup of the pepper mixture. Top each with another tortilla. Spoon 1-1/2 cups vegetables over each tortilla and sprinkle with Monterey Jack cheese. Top the last two tortillas with remaining beans and pepper mixture; place one on each stack. Sprinkle with cheddar cheese.

Bake at 375° for 10-15 minutes or until heated through and cheese is melted. Garnish with cilantro and olives. Cut into wedges. Serve with sour cream and picante sauce. **Yield:** 2 stacks (4-6 servings each).

Pizza Corn Dog Snacks

(Pictured at left)

Linda Knopp, Camas, Washington

I dress up frozen corn dogs to create these tasty bite-size treats. Just slice 'em and spread 'em with pizza sauce and other toppings for a fun snack for kids.

   1 package (16 ounces) frozen corn dogs,
       thawed
  1/2 cup pizza sauce
   3 tablespoons chopped ripe olives
   1 jar (4-1/2 ounces) sliced mushrooms, drained
  1/4 cup shredded mozzarella cheese

Remove stick from each corn dog; cut into 1-in. slices. Place on an ungreased baking sheet. Spread with pizza sauce. Top with olives, mushrooms and cheese. Bake at 350° for 15-20 minutes or until the cheese is melted and corn dogs are heated through. **Yield:** 30 snacks.

Cheesy Asparagus Bites

(Pictured at right)

Lois McAtee, Oceanside, California

When I used to manage a cafeteria, I would often cook up different snacks just for the staff. These tiny squares with a big asparagus flavor never lasted long and prompted lots of recipe requests.

- 1/2 cup diced onion
- 1 garlic clove, minced
- 2 tablespoons vegetable oil
- 2 cups (8 ounces) shredded sharp cheddar cheese
- 1/4 cup dry bread crumbs
- 2 tablespoons minced fresh parsley
- 1/4 teaspoon salt
- 1/4 teaspoon pepper
- 1/8 to 1/4 teaspoon dried oregano
- 1/8 teaspoon hot pepper sauce
- 4 eggs, beaten
- 1 pound fresh asparagus, trimmed and cut into 1/2-inch pieces

In a skillet, saute onion and garlic in oil until tender. Combine cheese, bread crumbs, parsley, salt, pepper, oregano and hot pepper sauce. Stir in the onion mixture and eggs. Cook asparagus in a small amount of water until crisp-tender, about 3-4 minutes; drain well. Stir into cheese mixture.

Pour into a greased 9-in. square baking pan. Bake at 350° for 30 minutes or until a knife inserted near the center comes out clean. Let stand for 15 minutes. Cut into small squares; serve warm. **Yield:** 5 dozen.

Sweet-Sour Chicken Dippers

(Pictured below left)

Kari Caven, Post Falls, Idaho

Since you can chop up all the ingredients the night before, this can be ready in about 30 minutes. I serve it as a snack or an appetizer...similar to chicken nuggets. I've substituted quail for the chicken, and it was delicious. Next, I may try pork!

- 1 can (8 ounces) crushed pineapple
- 1-1/2 cups sugar
- 1 can (14-1/2 ounces) diced tomatoes, undrained
- 1/2 cup vinegar
- 1/2 cup chopped onion
- 1/2 cup chopped green pepper
- 1 tablespoon soy sauce
- 1/4 teaspoon ground ginger
- 1 tablespoon cornstarch

BATTER:
- 1 cup all-purpose flour
- 1 cup cornstarch
- 2 teaspoons baking powder
- 2 teaspoons baking soda
- 2 teaspoons sugar
- 1-1/3 cups cold water
- Oil for deep-fat frying
- 1-1/2 pounds boneless skinless chicken breasts, cut into chunks

Drain pineapple, reserving juice. In a saucepan, combine sugar, tomatoes, vinegar, onion, green pepper, soy sauce, ginger and pineapple. Simmer for 20 minutes. In a bowl, combine cornstarch and the reserved pineapple juice until smooth; add to tomato mixture. Bring to a boil; boil and stir for 2 minutes or until slightly thickened. Remove from the heat; set aside.

In a bowl, combine the flour, cornstarch, baking powder, baking soda, sugar and water until smooth. In a deep-fat fryer, heat oil to 375°. Dip chicken pieces in batter; drop into oil and fry until golden brown and juices run clear, about 5 minutes. Serve immediately with sweet-sour sauce. **Yield:** 4 dozen appetizers.

Mozzarella Sticks

(Pictured below)

Mary Merchant, Barre, Vermont

I'm particularly fond of these tasty snacks because they're baked, not fried. Cheese is one of my family's favorite foods. Being of Italian descent, I cook often with ricotta and mozzarella cheeses.

    2 eggs
    1 tablespoon water
    1 cup dry bread crumbs
2-1/2 teaspoons Italian seasoning
  1/2 teaspoon garlic powder
  1/8 teaspoon pepper
   12 sticks string cheese
    3 tablespoons all-purpose flour
    1 tablespoon butter, melted
    1 cup marinara *or* spaghetti sauce, heated

In a small bowl, beat eggs and water. In a plastic bag, combine bread crumbs, Italian seasoning, garlic powder and pepper. Coat cheese sticks in flour, then dip in egg mixture and bread crumb mixture. Repeat egg and bread crumb coatings. Cover and chill for at least 4 hours or overnight.

Place on an ungreased baking sheet; drizzle with butter. Bake, uncovered, at 400° for 6-8 minutes or until heated through. Allow to stand for 3-5 minutes before serving. Use marinara or spaghetti sauce for dipping. **Yield:** 4-6 servings.

Editor's Note: Regular mozzarella cheese, cut into 4-in. x 1/2-in. sticks, can be substituted for the string cheese.

Toasted Zucchini Snacks

(Pictured above)

Jane Bone, Cape Coral, Florida

I added green pepper to this recipe I got years ago from a friend. I prepare this rich snack for company when zucchini is plentiful. Everyone seems to enjoy it—even those who say they don't care for zucchini.

   2 cups shredded zucchini
   1 teaspoon salt
1/2 cup mayonnaise
1/2 cup plain yogurt
1/4 cup grated Parmesan cheese
1/4 cup finely chopped green pepper
   4 green onions, thinly sliced
   1 garlic clove, minced
   1 teaspoon Worcestershire sauce
1/4 teaspoon hot pepper sauce
  36 slices snack rye bread

In a bowl, toss the zucchini and salt; let stand for 1 hour. Rinse and drain, pressing out excess liquid. Add the next eight ingredients; stir until combined. Spread a rounded teaspoonful on each slice of bread; place on a baking sheet. Bake at 375° for 10-12 minutes or until bubbly. Serve hot. **Yield:** 3 dozen.

Cold or Hot?

For potluck suppers, it's best to select a cold appetizer that can be prepared ahead and taken in a covered container. Hot appetizers requiring last-minute preparation are best served from your own kitchen.

Appetizer Meatballs

Nathalie Wiedmann-Guest, Caledon, Ontario

These are a favorite at parties and gatherings. The recipe is easy...and the meatballs can be made well ahead of time and frozen until needed.

- 2 eggs, lightly beaten
- 1 cup (4 ounces) shredded mozzarella cheese
- 1/2 cup dry bread crumbs
- 1/4 cup finely chopped onion
- 2 tablespoons grated Parmesan cheese
- 1 tablespoon ketchup
- 2 teaspoons Worcestershire sauce
- 1 teaspoon Italian seasoning
- 1 teaspoon dried basil
- 1 teaspoon salt
- 1/4 teaspoon pepper
- 2 pounds lean ground beef

SAUCE:
- 1 bottle (14 ounces) hot *or* regular ketchup
- 2 tablespoons cornstarch
- 1 jar (12 ounces) apple jelly
- 1 jar (12 ounces) currant jelly

In a bowl, combine the first 11 ingredients; add beef and mix well. Shape into 1-in. balls. Place on a rack in a shallow roasting pan. Bake at 350° for 10-15 minutes or until meat is no longer pink. Remove the meatballs and rack; drain.

Combine ketchup and cornstarch in roasting pan. Stir in jellies; add the meatballs. Cover and bake for 30 minutes. **Yield:** about 8 dozen.

Snack Pizzas

Margaret Allen, Abingdon, Virginia

This hearty snack is much like a sloppy joe sandwich, so it could be a meal in itself. Have knives and forks handy for folks to dig into these!

- 1 pound ground beef
- 1 medium onion, chopped
- 1/2 cup chopped green pepper
- 1 garlic clove, minced
- 1 can (6 ounces) tomato paste
- 3/4 cup water
- 4-1/2 teaspoons minced fresh oregano *or* 1-1/2 teaspoons dried oregano
- 1-1/2 teaspoons minced fresh thyme *or* 1/2 teaspoon dried thyme
- 1/2 teaspoon fennel seed
- 1/2 to 1 teaspoon garlic salt
- 36 slices snack rye bread

Grated Parmesan cheese

In a skillet, cook the beef, onion, green pepper and garlic over medium heat until meat is no longer pink; drain. Add tomato paste, water, oregano, thyme, fennel and garlic salt; cook over low heat until thickened, about 10 minutes.

Spread 1 tablespoonful on each slice of bread. Place on ungreased baking sheets; sprinkle with cheese. Bake at 350° for 8-10 minutes or until heated through. **Yield:** 3 dozen.

Twice-Baked New Potatoes

(Pictured above)

Susan Herbert, Aurora, Illinois

I've used these rich potatoes as both an appetizer and side dish. Guests seem to enjoy the distinctive taste of Monterey Jack cheese and basil. These satisfying mouthfuls are perfect for a late-afternoon or evening get-together when something a little heartier is needed.

- 1-1/2 pounds small red potatoes
- 2 to 3 tablespoons vegetable oil
- 1 cup (4 ounces) shredded Monterey Jack cheese
- 1/2 cup sour cream
- 1 package (3 ounces) cream cheese, softened
- 1/3 cup minced green onions
- 1 teaspoon dried basil
- 1 garlic clove, minced
- 1/2 teaspoon salt
- 1/4 to 1/2 teaspoon pepper
- 1/2 pound sliced bacon, cooked and crumbled

Pierce potatoes; rub skins with oil. Place in a baking pan. Bake, uncovered, at 400° for 50 minutes or until tender. Allow to cool to the touch.

In a mixing bowl, combine the Monterey Jack, sour cream, cream cheese, onions, basil, garlic, salt and pepper. Cut the potatoes in half; carefully scoop out the pulp, leaving a thin shell. Add pulp to the cheese mixture and mash; stir in bacon. Stuff potato shells. Broil for 7-8 minutes or until heated through. **Yield:** about 2 dozen.

Asparagus Ham Swirls

(Pictured above)

Nancy Ingersol, Midlothian, Illinois

I came across the recipe for this hot appetizer years ago and have made it many times to share with friends. Asparagus, ham and cheese combine into a fun finger food.

    16 fresh asparagus spears, trimmed
     3 tablespoons Dijon mustard
    16 thin slices fully cooked ham
    16 slices process Swiss cheese
     2 eggs, beaten
     1 cup dry bread crumbs
Vegetable oil

In a skillet, cook asparagus in a small amount of water until crisp-tender, about 6-8 minutes; drain well. Spread about 1 teaspoon of mustard on each ham slice. Top with one slice of cheese. Place an asparagus spear at one end (trim to fit if needed). Roll up each ham slice tightly; secure with three toothpicks. Dip ham rolls in egg, then roll in bread crumbs.

In an electric skillet, heat 1 in. of oil to 350°. Fry rolls, a few at a time, until golden brown, about 3-4 minutes. Drain on paper towels; keep warm. Cut each roll between toothpicks into three pieces. **Yield:** 4 dozen.

Almond Cheddar Appetizers

(Pictured at right)

Linda Thompson, Southampton, Ontario

I always try to have a supply of these on hand in the freezer. If guests drop in, I just pull some out and bake them.

     1 cup mayonnaise
     2 teaspoons Worcestershire sauce
     1 cup (4 ounces) shredded sharp cheddar cheese

     1 medium onion, chopped
    3/4 cup slivered almonds, chopped
     6 bacon strips, cooked and crumbled
     1 loaf (1 pound) French bread

In a bowl, combine mayonnaise and Worcestershire; stir in cheese, onion, almonds and bacon. Cut bread into 1/2-in. slices; spread with cheese mixture. Cut slices in half; place on a greased baking sheet. Bake at 400° for 8-10 minutes or until bubbly. **Yield:** about 4 dozen.

Editor's Note: Unbaked appetizers may be frozen. Place in a single layer on a baking sheet; freeze for 1 hour. Remove from the baking sheet and store in an airtight container for up to 2 months. When ready to use, place unthawed appetizers on a greased baking sheet. Bake at 400° for 10 minutes or until bubbly.

Cheese Boereg

Jean Ecos, Hartland, Wisconsin

Dinners in my home often start with this family-pleasing appetizer.

     1 egg, lightly beaten
     1 egg white, lightly beaten
     1 cup ricotta cheese
    1/4 cup minced fresh parsley
     4 cups (16 ounces) shredded mozzarella *or*
         Muenster cheese
     1 package (8 ounces) frozen phyllo dough, thawed
    1/2 cup butter, melted

In a bowl, combine the egg, egg white, ricotta and parsley. Stir in mozzarella; set aside. Unroll phyllo dough; cut the stack of sheets in half widthwise. Place one sheet of phyllo dough in a greased 13-in. x 9-in. x 2-in. baking pan; brush with butter. Repeat nine times (keep remaining dough covered with plastic wrap to avoid drying out).

Spread cheese mixture evenly over top. Layer with remaining dough, brushing butter on every other sheet. Bake at 350° for 25-30 minutes or until golden brown. Cut into squares or triangles. **Yield:** 16-20 appetizer servings.

Mini Corn Dogs

(Pictured above)

Geralyn Harrington, Floral Park, New York

For fun flavor, try this snack of cornmeal dough around mini hot dogs with a tangy dipping sauce.

- 1-2/3 cups all-purpose flour
- 1/3 cup cornmeal
- 3 teaspoons baking powder
- 1 teaspoon salt
- 3 tablespoons cold butter
- 1 tablespoon shortening
- 1 egg
- 3/4 cup milk
- 24 miniature hot dogs

HONEY MUSTARD SAUCE:
- 1/3 cup honey
- 1/3 cup prepared mustard
- 1 tablespoon molasses

In a large bowl, combine the first four ingredients. Cut in butter and shortening until mixture resembles coarse crumbs. Beat egg and milk; stir into dry ingredients until a soft dough forms.

Turn onto a lightly floured surface; knead 6-8 times or until smooth. Roll out to 1/4-in. thickness. Cut with a 2-1/4-in. biscuit cutter. Fold each dough circle over a hot dog and press edges to seal (dough will be sticky).

Place on greased baking sheets. Bake at 450° for 10-12 minutes or until golden brown. Combine sauce ingredients in a small bowl; mix well. Serve with the corn dogs. **Yield:** 2 dozen.

Cranberry Meatballs

Frances Venator, Ottumwa, Iowa

This is a versatile recipe that can be used either as an appetizer or as a main dish. You simply adjust the size of the meatballs. I like to serve it during the holidays as an appetizer. It satisfies appetites while guests await the main meal.

- 2 eggs, lightly beaten
- 1 cup crushed saltines (about 15 crackers)
- 1 medium onion, finely chopped
- 2 teaspoons salt
- 1/4 teaspoon pepper
- 1 pound ground beef
- 1 pound ground pork
- 2 cans (16 ounces *each*) wholeberry cranberry sauce
- 2 cans (10-3/4 ounces *each*) condensed tomato soup, undiluted
- 1 teaspoon prepared mustard

In a bowl, combine the eggs, crackers, onion, salt and pepper; crumble beef and pork over mixture and mix well. Shape into 1-in. meatballs. Place on a rack in a 15-in. x 10-in. x 1-in. baking pan. Bake at 400° for 15 minutes.

Meanwhile, combine the cranberry sauce, soup and mustard in a large saucepan. Bring to a boil. Reduce heat; add the meatballs. Simmer, uncovered, for 10 minutes or until heated through and meatballs are no longer pink. **Yield:** 5 dozen.

Editor's Note: To serve the meatballs as a main dish instead of an appetizer, make 1-1/4-inch balls and bake for 20 minutes.

1 pound boneless skinless chicken breasts,
   cut into 1-inch cubes
2 to 4 tablespoons vegetable oil
HONEY-MUSTARD SAUCE:
   3/4 cup mayonnaise
4-1/2 teaspoons honey
1-1/2 teaspoons Dijon mustard

In a large resealable plastic bag, combine the bread crumbs, sesame seeds and parsley; set aside. In a small bowl, combine the mayonnaise, onion powder, mustard and pepper. Coat chicken in mayonnaise mixture, then add to crumb mixture, a few pieces at a time, and shake to coat.

In a large skillet, saute chicken in oil in batches until juices run clear, adding additional oil as needed. In a small bowl, combine sauce ingredients. Serve with the chicken. **Yield:** 8-10 servings.

Sesame Chicken Bites

(Pictured above)

Kathy Green, Layton, New Jersey

So tender and tasty, these chicken appetizers are enhanced by a honey-mustard dipping sauce. These bites are among the favorites at my annual holiday open house.

1/2 cup dry bread crumbs
1/4 cup sesame seeds
  2 teaspoons minced fresh parsley
1/2 cup mayonnaise
  1 teaspoon onion powder
  1 teaspoon ground mustard
1/4 teaspoon pepper

Savory Party Bread

(Pictured below)

Kay Daly, Raleigh, North Carolina

It's impossible to stop nibbling on warm pieces of this cheesy, oniony bread. The sliced loaf fans out for a fun presentation.

  1 unsliced round loaf (1 pound) sourdough bread
  1 pound Monterey Jack cheese, sliced
1/2 cup butter, melted
1/2 cup chopped green onions
  2 to 3 teaspoons poppy seeds

Cut the bread lengthwise and crosswise without cutting through the bottom crust. Insert cheese between cuts. Combine butter, onions and poppy seeds; drizzle over the bread. Wrap in foil; place on a baking sheet. Bake at 350° for 15 minutes. Uncover; bake 10 minutes longer or until the cheese is melted. **Yield:** 6-8 servings.

Tiny Taco Meatballs

Joyce Markham, Belmond, Iowa

These meatballs may be tiny, but they're big on taste. Taco seasoning adds a tasty twist to these appetizers that my grandson gobbles up!

    2 eggs
    1 medium onion, finely chopped
    1 envelope taco seasoning
    1/2 teaspoon salt
    1/4 teaspoon pepper
    2 pounds ground beef
Taco sauce, optional

In a bowl, combine the first five ingredients. Add beef; mix well. Shape into 1-in. balls. Place in a foil-lined 15-in. x 10-in. x 1-in. baking pan. Bake at 400° for 14-18 minutes or until meat is no longer pink. Serve with taco sauce if desired. **Yield:** 14-16 servings.

Mozzarella Puffs

(Pictured below)

Joan Mousley Dziuba, Waupaca, Wisconsin

These savory, cheesy pizza-like biscuits go over great at my house. Since they're so quick to make, I can easily whip up a batch anytime.

    1 tube (7-1/2 ounces) refrigerated buttermilk
      biscuits
    1 teaspoon dried oregano
    1 block (2 to 3 ounces) mozzarella cheese
    2 tablespoons pizza sauce

Make an indentation in the center of each biscuit; sprinkle with oregano. Cut the mozzarella into 10 cubes, 3/4 in. each; place a cube in the center of each biscuit. Pinch dough tightly around cheese to seal. Place seam side down on an ungreased baking sheet. Spread pizza sauce over tops. Bake at 375° for 10-12 minutes or until golden brown. **Yield:** 10 servings.

Fried Jalapenos

(Pictured above)

DeLea Lonadier, Montgomery, Louisiana

Here's an appetizer that will heat up any gathering. Family and friends often request that I make these deep-fried jalapenos. I like them so much, though, I even make them to snack on when I don't have company.

    2 jars (12 ounces *each*) whole jalapeno peppers,
      drained*
    1 jar (5 ounces) olive-pimiento cheese spread
    3/4 cup all-purpose flour, *divided*
    6 tablespoons cornmeal, *divided*
    1/4 teaspoon salt
    1/4 teaspoon pepper
    1 cup buttermilk
Vegetable oil

Cut off stems and remove seeds from peppers. Stuff with cheese spread. Refrigerate for at least 2 hours. In a small bowl, combine 1/4 cup of flour, 2 tablespoons cornmeal, salt, pepper and buttermilk until smooth; set aside. In another bowl, combine remaining flour and cornmeal.

Dip stuffed peppers into buttermilk batter, then dredge in flour mixture. In an electric skillet or deep-fat fryer, heat oil to 375°. Fry peppers, two or three at a time, until they are golden brown. Drain on paper towels. **Yield:** 2 dozen.

***Editor's Note:** When cutting and seeding hot peppers, use rubber or plastic gloves to protect your hands; avoid touching your face.*

Ground Beef Snack Quiches

(Pictured below)

Stacey Atkinson, Rugby, North Dakota

My husband, Cory, farms, so supper can sometimes be quite late. A hearty appetizer like these meaty mini quiches is a perfect way to start the meal. They taste super made with ground beef, but I sometimes substitute bacon, ham, ground pork or sausage.

> 1/4 pound ground beef
> 1/8 to 1/4 teaspoon garlic powder
> 1/8 teaspoon pepper
> 1 cup biscuit/baking mix
> 1/4 cup cornmeal
> 1/4 cup cold butter
> 2 to 3 tablespoons boiling water
> 1 egg
> 1/2 cup half-and-half cream
> 1 tablespoon chopped green onion
> 1 tablespoon chopped sweet red pepper
> 1/8 to 1/4 teaspoon salt
> 1/8 to 1/4 teaspoon cayenne pepper
> 1/2 cup finely shredded cheddar cheese

In a saucepan over medium heat, cook beef, garlic powder and pepper until meat is no longer pink; drain and set aside. In a bowl, combine the biscuit mix and cornmeal; cut in butter. Add enough water to form a soft dough. Press onto the bottom and up the sides of greased miniature muffin cups. Place teaspoonfuls of beef mixture into each shell.

In a bowl, combine the egg, cream, onion, red pepper, salt and cayenne; pour over beef mixture. Sprinkle with cheese. Bake at 375° for 20 minutes or until a knife inserted near the center comes out clean. **Yield:** 1-1/2 dozen.

Black Bean Pizza

(Pictured above)

Janet Miller, Pittsburgh, Pennsylvania

Tomatoes and cheese give this black bean pizza traditional pizza flavor.

> 1 tube (10 ounces) refrigerated pizza dough
> 1 medium onion, chopped
> 1 garlic clove, minced
> 1 tablespoon vegetable oil
> 1/2 cup finely chopped zucchini
> 1 can (15 ounces) black beans, rinsed and drained
> 1 can (14-1/2 ounces) Italian diced tomatoes, undrained
> 1-1/2 cups (6 ounces) shredded Mexican-blend cheese, *divided*

Press dough into a greased 15-in. x 10-in. x 1-in. baking pan. Bake at 425° for 4-6 minutes or until crust just begins to brown. Meanwhile, in a skillet, saute the onion and garlic in oil until tender. Add zucchini; cook and stir for 1 minute. Add the beans and tomatoes; bring to a boil. Boil, uncovered, for 2 minutes; drain.

Sprinkle 2/3 cup of cheese over crust. Top with bean mixture and remaining cheese. Bake 8-10 minutes longer or until crust is browned and cheese is melted. **Yield:** 15-20 servings.

Pizza Party

Put out some small Italian bread shells and assorted toppings for kids. They can have fun making pizzas to suit their tastes, and you don't have to worry about them not liking the pizza you've prepared.

Sausage Wonton Stars

(Pictured at right)

Mary Thomas, North Lewisburg, Ohio

These fancy-looking appetizers are ideal when entertaining. The crunchy cups are stuffed with a cheesy pork sausage filling. We keep a few in the freezer so we can reheat them for late-night snacking.

- 1 package (12 ounces) wonton wrappers
- 1 pound bulk pork sausage
- 2 cups (8 ounces) shredded Colby cheese
- 1/2 medium green pepper, chopped
- 1/2 medium sweet red pepper, chopped
- 2 bunches green onions, sliced
- 1/2 cup ranch salad dressing

Lightly press wonton wrappers onto the bottom and up the sides of greased miniature muffin cups. Bake at 350° for 5 minutes or until edges are browned.

In a large skillet, cook sausage over medium heat until no longer pink; drain. Stir in the cheese, peppers, onions and salad dressing. Spoon a rounded tablespoonful into each wonton cup. Bake for 6-7 minutes or until heated through. **Yield:** about 4 dozen.

Guacamole Tortilla Snacks

Rhonda Black, Salinas, California

These zippy tortilla wedges always disappear quickly at parties. Mellow avocados and cheese balance the spicy jalapeno peppers.

- Oil for deep-fat frying
- 1 dozen corn tortillas (6 inches), quartered
- 3 ripe avocados, peeled and mashed
- 3 tablespoons mayonnaise
- 1 medium onion, diced
- 1 medium tomato, diced
- 2 jalapeno peppers, chopped*
- 2 cups (8 ounces) shredded Monterey Jack, Colby-Jack *or* cheddar cheese

In an electric skillet or deep-fat fryer, heat 1 in. of oil to 375°. Fry the tortilla wedges, a few at a time, until golden brown. Drain on paper towels. For guacamole, combine the avocados, mayonnaise, onion, tomato and jalapenos in a bowl.

Place tortillas on ungreased baking sheets. Top each with a tablespoonful of guacamole. Sprinkle with cheese. Broil 3-4 in. from heat for 2-3 minutes or until cheese is melted. Serve immediately. **Yield:** 4 dozen.

*Editor's Note: When cutting or seeding hot peppers, use rubber or plastic gloves to protect your hands. Avoid touching your face.

Sausage-Stuffed Mushrooms

Kathy Andrews, Winter Springs, Florida

These savory mushrooms taste a bit like pizza. They're a flavorful prelude to an Italian dinner.

- 24 large fresh mushrooms
- 1 pound bulk Italian sausage
- 1/2 cup chopped green onions
- 1 cup spaghetti sauce
- 1 cup (4 ounces) shredded mozzarella cheese

Remove mushroom stems; set caps aside. Chop stems; set aside. In a skillet, cook sausage over medium heat until no longer pink; remove with a slotted spoon.

In the drippings, saute onions and mushroom stems. Stir in spaghetti sauce and sausage. Stuff into mushroom caps. Sprinkle with cheese. Place in a greased 15-in. x 10-in. x 1-in. baking pan. Bake at 350° for 12-15 minutes or until cheese is melted. **Yield:** 2 dozen.

Shrimp and Cheddar Snacks

Margery Bryan, Royal City, Washington

If time is short, prepare the cheese spread ahead. When guests arrive, quickly assemble and bake.

- 2 cups (8 ounces) shredded cheddar cheese
- 1 cup mayonnaise
- 1 can (6 ounces) small shrimp, rinsed and drained
- 1 small onion, finely chopped
- 1/4 teaspoon garlic powder
- 42 slices snack rye bread, toasted

Combine cheese, mayonnaise, shrimp, onion and garlic powder; mix well. Spread 1 tablespoon over each slice of bread; place on ungreased baking sheets. Bake at 350° for 7-9 minutes or until bubbly. Serve hot. **Yield:** 3-1/2 dozen.

Corn Bread Pizza Wheels

(Pictured below)

Patrick Lucas, Cochran, Georgia

This hearty, colorful snack looks like you fussed, but it's really simple to make. Even folks who don't normally care for Mexican food dig right into this pizza!

- 1 pound ground beef
- 1 can (16 ounces) kidney beans, rinsed and drained
- 1 can (8 ounces) tomato sauce
- 4 teaspoons chili powder
- 1 jar (4 ounces) diced pimientos, drained
- 1 can (4 ounces) chopped green chilies, drained
- 1 cup (4 ounces) shredded cheddar cheese
- 2 tablespoons cornmeal
- 2 tubes (11-1/2 ounces *each*) refrigerated corn bread twists

Shredded lettuce, sliced tomatoes and sour cream

In a skillet, cook beef over medium heat until no longer pink; drain. Add beans, tomato sauce and chili powder. Simmer, uncovered, until liquid has evaporated. Remove from the heat; cool. Stir in the pimientos, chilies and cheese; set aside.

Sprinkle two greased 14-in. pizza pans with cornmeal. Pat corn bread dough into a 14-in. circle on each pan. With a sharp knife, cut a 7-in. "X" in the center of the dough. Cut another 7-in. "X" to form eight pie-shaped wedges in the center.

Spoon the filling around edge of dough. Fold points of dough over filling; tuck under ring and pinch to seal (filling will be visible). Bake at 400° for 15-20 minutes or until golden brown. Fill center of pizza with lettuce, tomatoes and sour cream. **Yield:** 2 pizzas (8 servings each).

Spinach Turnovers

Jean von Bereghy, Oconomowoc, Wisconsin

The flaky cream cheese pastry adds sensational texture to these hot appetizers—and just wait until you taste the wonderful filling.

- 2 packages (8 ounces *each*) cream cheese, softened
- 3/4 cup butter, softened
- 2-1/2 cups all-purpose flour
- 1/2 teaspoon salt

FILLING:
- 5 bacon strips, diced
- 1/4 cup finely chopped onion
- 2 garlic cloves, minced
- 1 package (10 ounces) frozen chopped spinach, thawed and well drained
- 1 cup small-curd cottage cheese
- 1/4 teaspoon salt
- 1/4 teaspoon pepper
- 1/8 teaspoon ground nutmeg
- 1 egg, beaten

Salsa, optional

In a mixing bowl, beat cream cheese and butter until smooth. Combine flour and salt; gradually add to creamed mixture (dough will be stiff). Turn onto a floured surface; gently knead 10 times. Cover and refrigerate at least 2 hours.

In a skillet, cook bacon until crisp. Remove bacon; reserve 1 tablespoon drippings. Saute onion and garlic in drippings until tender. Remove from heat; stir in bacon, spinach, cottage cheese and seasonings. Cool.

On a lightly floured surface, roll dough to 1/8-in. thickness. Cut into 3-in. circles; brush edges with egg. Place 1 heaping teaspoon of filling on each circle. Fold over; seal edges. Prick tops with a fork. Brush with egg. Bake at 400° for 10-12 minutes or until golden brown. Serve with salsa if desired. **Yield:** about 4 dozen.

if desired. Microwave 40-60 seconds longer or until cheese is melted. **Yield:** 10-12 servings.

Editor's Note: This recipe was tested in an 850-watt microwave.

Honey-Mustard Turkey Meatballs

(Pictured below)

Bonnie Durkin, Nescopeck, Pennsylvania

I serve this appetizer often during the holidays. These tangy meatballs can be prepared ahead and frozen, so even drop-in guests can be treated to a hot snack.

1 egg, lightly beaten
3/4 cup crushed butter-flavored crackers
1/2 cup shredded mozzarella cheese
1/4 cup chopped onion
1/2 teaspoon ground ginger
6 tablespoons Dijon mustard, *divided*
1 pound ground turkey
1-1/4 cups unsweetened pineapple juice
1/4 cup chopped green pepper
2 tablespoons honey
1 tablespoon cornstarch
1/4 teaspoon onion powder

In a bowl, combine egg, cracker crumbs, cheese, onion, ginger and 3 tablespoons mustard. Add turkey and mix well. Form into 30 balls, 1 in. each. Place in a greased 13-in. x 9-in. x 2-in. baking dish. Bake, uncovered, at 350° for 20-25 minutes or until juices run clear.

In a saucepan, combine pineapple juice, green pepper, honey, cornstarch and onion powder; bring to a boil, stirring constantly. Cook and stir 2 minutes more; reduce heat. Stir in remaining mustard until smooth. Brush meatballs with about 1/4 cup sauce and return to the oven for 10 minutes. Serve remaining sauce as a dip for meatballs. **Yield:** 2-1/2 dozen.

Feta Bruschetta

(Pictured above and on front cover)

Stacey Rinehart, Eugene, Oregon

You won't believe the compliments you'll receive when you greet guests with these appetizers. Each crispy bite offers savory tastes of feta cheese, tomatoes, basil and garlic.

1/4 cup butter, melted
1/4 cup olive oil
10 slices French bread (1 inch thick)
1 package (4 ounces) crumbled feta cheese
2 to 3 garlic cloves, minced
1 tablespoon minced fresh basil *or* 1 teaspoon dried basil
1 large tomato, seeded and chopped

In a bowl, combine butter and oil; brush onto both sides of bread. Place on a baking sheet. Bake at 350° for 8-10 minutes or until lightly browned on top. Combine the feta cheese, garlic and basil; sprinkle over toast. Top with tomato. Bake 8-10 minutes longer or until heated through. Serve warm. **Yield:** 10 appetizers.

Speedy Pizza Rings

Karen Hope, Miller, Missouri

If your family likes pizza, they're going to love these pizza-flavored snacks featuring zucchini.

2 medium zucchini (about 2-inch diameter),
cut into 1/4-inch slices
1 can (8 ounces) pizza sauce
1 package (3 ounces) sliced pepperoni
1 cup (4 ounces) shredded mozzarella cheese
Sliced jalapeno peppers and ripe olives, optional

Arrange zucchini in a single layer on a large microwave-safe plate coated with nonstick cooking spray. Microwave, uncovered, on high for 3 minutes. Spread 1 teaspoon pizza sauce on each zucchini round; top each with a slice of pepperoni. Heat, uncovered, for 2 minutes. Sprinkle each with cheese, jalapenos and olives

Pizza Roll-Ups

(Pictured above)

Donna Klettke, Wheatland, Missouri

Since receiving this recipe through 4-H, I've served it as a regular after-school snack. These bite-size pizza treats, made with refrigerated crescent rolls, are especially good served with spaghetti sauce for dipping.

- 1/2 pound ground beef
- 1 can (8 ounces) tomato sauce
- 1/2 cup shredded mozzarella cheese
- 1/2 teaspoon dried oregano
- 2 tubes (8 ounces *each*) refrigerated crescent rolls

In a skillet, cook beef over medium heat until no longer pink; drain. Remove from the heat. Add tomato sauce, mozzarella cheese and oregano; mix well. Separate crescent dough into eight rectangles, pinching seams together.

Place about 3 tablespoons of meat mixture along one long side of each rectangle. Roll up, jelly-roll style, starting with a long side. Cut each roll into three pieces. Place, seam side down, 2 in. apart on greased baking sheets. Bake at 375° for 15 minutes or until golden brown. **Yield:** 2 dozen.

Ham and Swiss Snacks

Beth Gambro, Yorkville, Illinois

Following a ball game or for a fun after-school treat, ravenous teenagers can prepare this satisfying snack in a jiffy. It's an unusual but delicious combination of ham, cheese and apples on a no-fuss crust.

- 2 tubes (8 ounces *each*) refrigerated crescent rolls
- 2 tablespoons prepared mustard
- 2 tablespoons dried parsley flakes
- 2 tablespoons finely chopped onion
- 1 tablespoon butter, softened
- 1 cup chopped peeled tart apple
- 1 cup chopped fully cooked ham
- 3/4 cup shredded Swiss cheese
- 2 tablespoons grated Parmesan cheese

Unroll crescent dough; pat onto the bottom and up the sides of an ungreased 15-in. x 10-in. x 1-in. baking pan. Seal seams and perforations. Bake at 375° for 10-12 minutes or until lightly browned.

Combine mustard, parsley, onion and butter; spread over crust. Sprinkle with apple, ham and cheeses. Bake 5-10 minutes longer or until cheese is melted. Cut into squares. **Yield:** 2 dozen.

Savory Rye Snacks

(Pictured below)

Connie Simon, Reed City, Michigan

I make the flavorful spread ahead of time and refrigerate it. Then all I have to do to have a quick snack is put it on the rye bread and bake.

- 1 cup sliced green onions
- 1 cup mayonnaise
- 1 cup (4 ounces) shredded Monterey Jack cheese
- 1 cup (4 ounces) shredded cheddar cheese
- 1 can (4 ounces) mushroom stems and pieces, drained
- 1/2 cup chopped ripe olives
- 1/2 cup chopped pimiento-stuffed green olives
- 1 loaf (1 pound) cocktail rye bread

In a bowl, combine the first seven ingredients. Spread on bread slices and place on ungreased baking sheets. Bake at 350° for 8-10 minutes or until bubbly. **Yield:** about 4 dozen.

Orange-Pecan Hot Wings

(Pictured at right)
June Jones, Hudson, Florida

We like to use oranges and orange juice in lots of different ways—we even have an orange tree in our backyard. These chicken wings are a fun appetizer.

    3 pounds whole chicken wings*
    3 eggs
    1 can (6 ounces) frozen orange juice concentrate,
      thawed
    2 tablespoons water
    1 cup all-purpose flour
    1/2 cup finely chopped pecans
    1/2 cup butter, melted
RED HOT SAUCE:
    2 cups ketchup
    3/4 cup packed brown sugar
    2 to 3 tablespoons hot pepper sauce

Cut chicken wings into three pieces; discard wing tips. In a bowl, whisk eggs, orange juice concentrate and water. In another bowl or a resealable plastic bag, combine flour and pecans.

Dip wings in egg mixture, then roll or toss in flour mixture. Pour butter into a 15-in. x 10-in. x 1-in. baking pan. Arrange wings in a single layer in pan. Bake, uncovered, at 375° for 25 minutes.

Meanwhile, combine sauce ingredients. Spoon half over the wings; turn. Top with remaining sauce. Bake 30 minutes longer or until meat juices run clear. **Yield: 8-10 servings.**

***Editor's Note:** 3 pounds of uncooked chicken wing sections can be substituted for the whole chicken wings. Omit the first step of the directions.

Chicken Quesadillas

Linda Miller, Klamath Falls, Oregon

Tender homemade tortillas make this savory snack taste extra-special.

      4 cups all-purpose flour
  1-1/2 teaspoons salt
    1/2 teaspoon baking powder
      1 cup shortening
  1-1/4 cups warm water
      1 cup *each* shredded cheddar, mozzarella and
          pepper Jack cheese
      2 cups diced cooked chicken
      1 cup sliced green onions
      1 cup sliced ripe olives
      1 can (4 ounces) chopped green chilies, drained
Salsa and sour cream

In a bowl, combine the flour, salt and baking powder. Cut in shortening until crumbly. Add enough warm water, stirring, until mixture forms a ball. Let stand for 10 minutes. Divide into 28 portions. On a lightly floured surface, roll each portion into a 7-in. circle. Cook on a lightly greased griddle for 1-1/2 to 2 minutes on each side, breaking any bubbles with a toothpick if necessary. Keep warm.

In a bowl, combine the cheeses. For each quesadilla, place a tortilla on the griddle; sprinkle with about 2 tablespoons cheese mixture, 2 tablespoons chicken, 1 tablespoon onions, 1 tablespoon olives and 1 teaspoon chilies. Top with 1 tablespoon cheese mixture and another tortilla.

Cook for 30-60 seconds; turn and cook 30 seconds longer or until cheese is melted. Cut into wedges. Serve with salsa and sour cream. **Yield: 14 quesadillas.**

Chili Cheese Tart

Rachel Nash, Pascagoula, Mississippi

When I fix this flavorful appetizer, I have to keep an eye out for sneaky fingers. My family just can't resist sampling the cheesy wedges. They're delicious topped with salsa and sour cream.

    1 package (15 ounces) refrigerated pie pastry
      (2 sheets)
    1 can (4 ounces) chopped green chilies, drained
    1 cup (4 ounces) shredded cheddar cheese
    1 cup (4 ounces) shredded Monterey Jack cheese
    1/4 teaspoon chili powder
Salsa and sour cream

Place one sheet of pie pastry on an ungreased pizza pan or baking sheet. Sprinkle chilies and cheeses over pastry to within 1/2 in. of edges. Top with remaining pastry; seal edges and prick top with a fork.

Sprinkle with chili powder. Bake at 450° for 10-15 minutes or until golden brown. Cool for 10 minutes before cutting into wedges. Serve with salsa and sour cream. **Yield: 10-14 servings.**

Baked Egg Rolls

(Pictured below)

Barbra Lierman, Lyons, Nebraska

My family enjoys a variety of different foods including these crisp egg rolls. They're packed with tasty ingredients and are also low in fat.

 Uses less fat, sugar or salt. Includes Nutritional Analysis and Diabetic Exchanges.

- 2 cups grated carrots
- 1 can (14 ounces) bean sprouts, drained
- 1/2 cup chopped water chestnuts
- 1/4 cup chopped green pepper
- 1/4 cup chopped green onions
- 1 garlic clove, minced
- 2 cups finely diced cooked chicken
- 4 teaspoons cornstarch
- 1 tablespoon water
- 1 tablespoon reduced-sodium soy sauce
- 1 teaspoon vegetable oil
- 1 teaspoon brown sugar
- Pinch cayenne pepper
- 16 egg roll wrappers*

Coat a large skillet with nonstick cooking spray; add the first six ingredients. Cook and stir over medium heat until vegetables are crisp-tender, about 3 minutes. Add chicken; heat through. In a small bowl, combine cornstarch, water, soy sauce, oil, brown sugar and cayenne until smooth; stir into chicken mixture. Bring to a boil. Cook and stir for 2 minutes; remove from the heat.

Spoon 1/4 cup of chicken mixture on the bottom third of one egg roll wrapper; fold sides toward center and roll tightly. Place seam side down on a baking sheet coated with nonstick cooking spray. Repeat with remaining

wrappers and filling. Spray tops of egg rolls with nonstick cooking spray. Bake at 425° for 10-15 minutes or until lightly browned. **Yield:** 8 servings.

Nutritional Analysis: One serving (2 egg rolls) equals 261 calories, 518 mg sodium, 27 mg cholesterol, 45 g carbohydrate, 13 g protein, 3 g fat. **Diabetic Exchanges:** 3 starch, 1 lean meat.

*Editor's Note: Fill egg roll wrappers one at a time, keeping the others covered until ready to use.

Salmon Tartlets

(Pictured above)

Carolyn Kyzer, Alexander, Arkansas

These make great appetizers, but sometimes I forgo the crust and make the filling into a loaf for a family meal.

- 1/2 cup butter, softened
- 1 package (3 ounces) cream cheese, softened
- 1 cup all-purpose flour
- FILLING:
- 2 eggs
- 1/2 cup milk
- 1 tablespoon butter, melted
- 1 teaspoon lemon juice
- 1/2 cup dry bread crumbs
- 1-1/2 teaspoons dried parsley flakes
- 1/2 teaspoon rubbed sage
- 1/2 teaspoon salt
- 1/4 teaspoon pepper
- 1 can (14-3/4 ounces) salmon, drained and bones removed
- 1 green onion, sliced

In a mixing bowl, beat butter, cream cheese and flour until smooth. Shape tablespoonfuls of dough into balls; press onto the bottom and up the sides of greased miniature muffin cups.

In a bowl, combine eggs, milk, butter and lemon juice. Stir in crumbs, parsley, sage, salt and pepper. Fold in salmon and onion. Spoon into shells. Bake at 350° for 30-35 minutes or until browned. **Yield:** 2 dozen.

Cheese Wedges

(Pictured at right)

Jennifer Eilts, Omaha, Nebraska

These easy cheesy treats are a hit at evening gatherings. They're great for dipping.

> 1 package (7 ounces) extra sharp cheddar cheese
> 1/3 cup seasoned dry bread crumbs
> 1/2 teaspoon crushed red pepper flakes, optional
> 1 egg
> 1 can (8 ounces) pizza sauce, warmed

Cut cheese into 1/2-in. slices; cut each slice in half diagonally. In a shallow bowl, combine bread crumbs and red pepper flakes if desired. In another bowl, beat egg. Dip cheese triangles into egg, then in crumb mixture. Place on a greased baking sheet. Broil 4 in. from heat for 2-3 minutes or until browned and cheese begins to melt. Serve warm with pizza sauce. **Yield:** 6 servings.

Apricot Wraps

(Pictured below)

Jane Ashworth, Beavercreek, Ohio

I accumulated a large recipe collection from around the world while my husband served in the Air Force for 25 years. This mouth-watering appetizer is one of our favorites, and we enjoy sharing it with friends.

> 1 package (14 ounces) dried apricots
> 1/2 cup whole almonds
> 1 pound sliced bacon

> 1/4 cup plum *or* apple jelly
> 2 tablespoons soy sauce

Fold each apricot around an almond. Cut bacon strips into thirds; wrap a strip around each apricot and secure with a toothpick. Place on two ungreased 15-in. x 10-in. x 1-in. baking pans. Bake, uncovered, at 375° for 25 minutes or until bacon is crisp, turning once.

In a small saucepan, combine jelly and soy sauce; cook and stir over low heat for 5 minutes or until warmed and smooth. Remove apricots to paper towels; drain. Serve with sauce for dipping. **Yield:** about 4-1/2 dozen.

Festive Sausage Cups

(Pictured below)

Gail Watkins, South Bend, Indiana

When I use prepared pie crust for this recipe, it's even easier to form and fill these individual sausage cups. They are a savory and filling snack.

Pastry for double-crust pie (9 inches)
- 1 pound bulk hot pork sausage
- 6 green onions, chopped
- 1 tablespoon butter
- 1/2 cup chopped canned mushrooms
- 1/4 cup thinly sliced stuffed olives
- 3/4 teaspoon salt
- 1/4 teaspoon pepper
- 1/4 cup all-purpose flour
- 2 cups heavy whipping cream
- 1 cup (4 ounces) shredded Swiss cheese

Chopped stuffed olives

On a lightly floured surface, roll pastry to 1/8-in. thickness. Cut with a 2-1/2-in. round cookie cutter. Press onto the bottom and up the sides of greased miniature muffin cups. Bake at 400° for 6-8 minutes or until lightly browned. Remove from pans to cool on wire racks.

In a skillet, brown sausage; drain well and set aside. In the same skillet, saute onions in butter until tender. Add mushrooms, sliced olives, salt and pepper. Sprinkle with flour. Add cream; bring to a boil, stirring constantly. Stir in sausage. Reduce heat; simmer until thickened, about 5-10 minutes, stirring constantly.

Spoon into pastry cups; sprinkle with cheese. Place on ungreased baking sheets. Bake at 350° for 10 minutes or until cheese is melted. Garnish with chopped olives. Serve hot. **Yield:** 4 dozen.

Mini Mexican Quiches

(Pictured above right)

Linda Hendrix, Moundville, Missouri

This fun finger food is great for a brunch, shower, party or whenever you want to munch a yummy treat.

- 1/2 cup butter, softened
- 1 package (3 ounces) cream cheese, softened
- 1 cup all-purpose flour
- 1 cup (4 ounces) shredded Monterey Jack cheese
- 1 can (4 ounces) chopped green chilies, drained
- 2 eggs
- 1/2 cup heavy whipping cream
- 1/4 teaspoon salt
- 1/8 teaspoon pepper

In a small mixing bowl, cream butter and cream cheese. Add flour; beat until well blended. Shape into 24 balls; cover and refrigerate for 1 hour. Press balls onto the bottom and up the sides of greased miniature muffin cups. Sprinkle a rounded teaspoonful of cheese and 1/2 teaspoon of chilies into each shell.

In a bowl, beat eggs, cream, salt and pepper. Spoon into shells. Bake at 350° for 30-35 minutes or until golden brown. Let stand for 5 minutes before serving. Refrigerate leftovers. **Yield:** 2 dozen.

Parmesan Chicken Wings

Ellen Montei, Caro, Michigan

Over the many years I've been cooking, I've had my share of flops, but these well-seasoned chicken wings have never failed me. Crisp and cheesy, they're outstanding as an appetizer and always draw a crowd.

- 16 whole chicken wings
- 3/4 cup finely crushed butter-flavored crackers
- 3/4 cup grated Parmesan cheese
- 1 teaspoon dried basil
- 3/4 teaspoon garlic salt
- 1/4 cup butter, melted

Cut chicken wings into three sections; discard wing tips. In a small bowl, combine cracker crumbs, Parmesan cheese, basil and garlic salt. Dip wings in butter, then roll in crumb mixture. Place in a single layer on greased baking sheets. Bake at 375° for 35-40 minutes or until golden brown and juices run clear. **Yield:** 8-10 servings.

Crispy Chicken Wontons

Connie Blesse, Auberry, California

Served with a choice of plum or sweet-sour sauces, these crunchy appetizers are always a big hit at parties. They're so popular that my family has even requested them as a main dish for dinner.

- 3 cups finely chopped cooked chicken
- 1/2 cup shredded carrot
- 1/4 cup finely chopped water chestnuts
- 2 teaspoons cornstarch
- 1 tablespoon water
- 1 tablespoon soy sauce
- 1/2 to 1 teaspoon ground ginger
- 1 package (16 ounces) wonton wrappers*
- 2 tablespoons butter, melted
- 1 tablespoon vegetable oil

Plum *or* sweet-sour sauce

In a bowl, combine chicken, carrot and water chestnuts. In another bowl, combine cornstarch, water, soy sauce and ginger until smooth. Add to chicken mixture; toss to coat. Spoon 1 teaspoon of filling in the center of each wonton wrapper.

Moisten the edges with water. Bring opposite points together; pinch to seal. Place filled wontons on greased baking sheets. Combine butter and oil; brush over the wontons. Bake at 375° for 10-12 minutes or until golden brown. Serve with plum or sweet-sour sauce. **Yield:** about 4 dozen.

***Editor's Note:** Fill wonton wrappers a few at a time, keeping the others covered until ready to use.

Tomato-Onion Phyllo Pizza

(Pictured at right)

Neta Cohen, Bedford, Virginia

With a delicate crust and lots of lovely tomatoes on top, this dish is a special one to serve to guests. I make it often when fresh garden tomatoes are in season. It freezes well unbaked, so I can keep one on hand to pop in the oven for a quick snack for drop-in company.

- 5 tablespoons butter, melted
- 7 sheets phyllo dough (18 inches x 14 inches)
- 7 tablespoons grated Parmesan cheese, *divided*
- 1 cup (4 ounces) shredded mozzarella cheese
- 1 cup thinly sliced onion
- 7 to 9 plum tomatoes (about 1-1/4 pounds), sliced
- 1-1/2 teaspoons minced fresh oregano *or* 1/2 teaspoon dried oregano
- 1 teaspoon minced fresh thyme *or* 1/4 teaspoon dried thyme

Salt and pepper to taste

Brush a 15-in. x 10-in. x 1-in. baking pan with some of the melted butter. Lay a sheet of phyllo in the pan, folding edges in to fit (keep the remaining dough covered with waxed paper to avoid drying out). Brush the dough with butter and sprinkle with 1 tablespoon Parmesan cheese. Repeat layers five times, folding edges for each layer.

Top with remaining dough, folding edges to fit pan; brush with remaining butter. Sprinkle with mozzarella cheese; arrange onion and tomatoes over the cheese. Sprinkle with oregano, thyme, salt, pepper and remaining Parmesan. Bake at 375° for 20-25 minutes or until edges are golden brown. **Yield:** 28 slices.

Cheesy Olive Snacks

Dorothy Anderson, Ottawa, Kansas

Olive lovers will snap up these chewy, delicious appetizers. They're easy since the topping can be made ahead and they bake for only 7 minutes.

- 1 cup (4 ounces) shredded mozzarella cheese
- 1 cup (4 ounces) shredded cheddar cheese
- 1 can (4-1/4 ounces) chopped ripe olives, drained
- 1/2 cup mayonnaise
- 1/3 cup chopped green onions

Triscuit crackers

In a bowl, combine the mozzarella and cheddar cheeses, olives, mayonnaise and onions. Spread on crackers. Place on an ungreased baking sheet. Bake at 375° for 7 minutes or until cheese is melted. Serve immediately. **Yield:** about 4 dozen.

On a lightly floured surface, roll out each biscuit into a 4-in. circle; brush with butter. Combine Parmesan cheese and oregano; sprinkle over butter. Place a sausage link in the center of each; roll up. Cut each widthwise into four pieces; insert a toothpick into each. Place on an ungreased baking sheet. Bake at 375° for 8-10 minutes or until golden brown. **Yield:** 40 appetizers.

Chicken Meatball Appetizers

Norma Snider, Chambersburg, Pennsylvania

These nicely seasoned chicken meatballs are a crowd-pleasing change of pace on the appetizer tray. They're great plain or dipped in mustard.

✓ **Uses less fat, sugar or salt. Includes Nutritional Analysis and Diabetic Exchanges.**

  2-1/2 cups minced cooked chicken breast
   3 tablespoons finely chopped onion
   3 tablespoons finely chopped celery
   2 tablespoons finely chopped carrot
   2 tablespoons dry bread crumbs
   1 egg white
  1/2 teaspoon poultry seasoning
Pinch pepper

In a bowl, combine all ingredients; mix well. Shape into 3/4-in. balls; place on a baking sheet that has been coated with nonstick cooking spray. Bake at 400° for 8-10 minutes or until lightly browned. **Yield:** about 2-1/2 dozen.

Nutritional Analysis: One serving (3 meatballs) equals 42 calories, 23 mg sodium, 21 mg cholesterol, 2 g carbohydrate, 6 g protein, 1 g fat. **Diabetic Exchange:** 1 very lean meat.

Jalapeno Pepper Appetizers

(Pictured above)
Peggy Roberts, Lockney, Texas

These appetizers are so easy to make and they taste so good. I have to warn you that eating them is habit-forming!

 10 medium fresh jalapeno peppers*
  4 ounces cream cheese, softened
 10 bacon strips, halved

Cut peppers in half lengthwise; remove seeds, stems and center membrane. Stuff each half with about 2 teaspoons of cream cheese. Wrap with bacon and secure with a toothpick. Place on a broiler rack that has been coated with nonstick cooking spray. Bake at 350° for 20-25 minutes or until bacon is crisp. Remove toothpicks. Serve immediately. **Yield:** 20 appetizers.

*Editor's Note: When cutting or seeding hot peppers, use rubber or plastic gloves to protect your hands. Avoid touching your face.

Sausage Biscuit Bites

(Pictured at right)
Audrey Marler, Kokomo, Indiana

I sometimes bake these delightful little morsels the night before, refrigerate them, then put them in the slow cooker in the morning so my husband can share them with his co-workers. They're always gone in a hurry.

   1 tube (7-1/2 ounces) refrigerated buttermilk
     biscuits
   1 tablespoon butter, melted
4-1/2 teaspoons grated Parmesan cheese
   1 teaspoon dried oregano
   1 package (8 ounces) brown-and-serve sausage
     links

Asparagus Roll-Ups

(Pictured at right)
Clara Nenstiel, Pampa, Texas

These roll-ups are simply divine. A friend shared the recipe after serving them at a church brunch, where they disappeared fast. They make a unique finger food, a side dish at supper or a lovely lunch served with soup.

- 16 fresh asparagus spears
- 16 slices sandwich bread, crusts removed
- 1 package (8 ounces) cream cheese, softened
- 8 bacon strips, cooked and crumbled
- 2 tablespoons minced fresh *or* dried chives
- 1/4 cup butter, melted
- 3 tablespoons grated Parmesan cheese

Place asparagus in a skillet with a small amount of water and cook until crisp-tender, about 6-8 minutes. Drain and set aside. Flatten bread with a rolling pin. Combine the cream cheese, bacon and chives; spread 1 tablespoonful on each slice of bread. Top each with an asparagus spear.

Roll up tightly, then place seam side down on a greased baking sheet. Brush with melted butter and sprinkle with Parmesan cheese. Cut roll-ups in half. Bake at 400° for 10-12 minutes or until lightly browned. **Yield:** 32 appetizers.

Hawaiian Egg Rolls

Terri Wheeler, Vadnais Heights, Minnesota

An avid cook, I am constantly trying to come up with recipes for using leftovers. This one gives a whole new twist to extra ham. My two children think these egg rolls are great, and they freeze well. I simply thaw as many as needed and bake them for a quick snack.

- 10 fresh spinach leaves, julienned
- 1/2 teaspoon ground ginger
- 2 tablespoons olive oil
- 1/2 pound fully cooked ham, coarsely ground (2 cups)
- 4 water chestnuts, chopped
- 1/4 cup undrained crushed pineapple
- 2 tablespoons chopped green onions
- 1 tablespoon soy sauce
- 7 egg roll wrappers
Vegetable oil for frying
Sweet-sour sauce

In a saucepan, saute the spinach and ginger in oil for 1-2 minutes. In a bowl, combine the ham, water chestnuts, pineapple, onions and soy sauce. Stir in the spinach mixture.

Place 3 tablespoons of ham mixture in the center of each egg roll wrapper. Fold bottom corner over filling; fold sides over filling toward center. Moisten remaining corner with water; roll up tightly to seal.

In an electric skillet, heat 1 in. of oil to 375°. Fry egg rolls for 2 minutes on each side or until golden brown. Drain on paper towels. Serve with sweet-sour sauce. **Yield:** 7 egg rolls.

Sweet-Hot Sausage Meatballs

Claire Stryker, Delta, Utah

These good-tasting sausage meatballs seem to disappear before anything else on the table or buffet. They have a delightful tang with a bit of crunch from the water chestnuts. I've used the recipe when entertaining for over 20 years because it's so easy to do and comes out perfect every time.

- 2 cans (8 ounces *each*) water chestnuts, drained
- 1 pound bulk pork sausage
- 1 pound bulk hot pork sausage
- 1/4 cup cornstarch
- 1 cup maple syrup
- 2/3 cup red wine vinegar
- 1/4 cup soy sauce

In a blender or food processor, process water chestnuts until minced. Transfer to a bowl; add sausage. Mix well. Shape into 1-in. balls. Place in ungreased 15-in. x 10-in. x 1-in. baking pans. Bake, uncovered, at 350° for 20-25 minutes or until meat is no longer pink.

Meanwhile, in a saucepan, combine cornstarch, syrup, vinegar and soy sauce; stir until smooth. Bring to a boil; cook and stir for 2 minutes or until thickened and bubbly. Drain meatballs; add to sauce and heat through. **Yield:** 12-14 servings.

Making Meatballs

To make meatballs of equal size, pat meat mixture into a 1-inch-thick rectangle. With a knife, cut rectangle into the same number of squares as meatballs needed. Gently roll each square into a ball.

Sesame Chicken Strips

(Pictured above)

Teri Rasey, Cadillac, Michigan

These tasty chicken strips dipped in the lightly sweet sauce are a wonderful finger food. They go over really well at outdoor summer gatherings. This recipe puts a new twist on fried chicken—a staple at most picnics.

    1 cup mayonnaise
    2 teaspoons dried minced onion
    2 teaspoons ground mustard
    1 cup crushed butter-flavored crackers
1/2 cup sesame seeds
    2 pounds boneless skinless chicken breasts
SAUCE:
    1 cup mayonnaise
    2 tablespoons honey

In a bowl, combine the mayonnaise, onion and mustard. In another bowl, combine the crackers and sesame seeds. Cut the chicken lengthwise into 1/4-in. strips. Dip the strips into mayonnaise mixture, then into the sesame seed mixture.

Place in a single layer on a large greased baking sheet. Bake at 425° for 15-18 minutes or until the juices run clear. Combine the sauce ingredients and serve with the chicken strips. **Yield:** 10-12 appetizer servings.

Chili Cheese Tidbits

Karen Ann Bland, Gove, Kansas

When I had three active teenagers at home, I heard, "Mom, what's for a snack?" 365 days a year. We all love spicy finger foods, and this recipe fills the bill.

    3 cans (4 ounces *each*) chopped green chilies, drained
    3 eggs, lightly beaten
    2 cups (8 ounces) shredded cheddar cheese
Triscuits *or* other crackers

Spread chilies onto the bottom of a greased 8-in. square baking pan. Pour eggs over chilies; sprinkle with cheese. Bake, uncovered, at 350° for 20-25 minutes or until cheese is melted. Cool slightly; cut into squares and serve on crackers. Refrigerate leftovers. **Yield:** 3 dozen.

Onion Rye Appetizers

Vicki Wolf, Aurora, Ohio

I take these hearty appetizers to every party we attend and always bring home an empty tray.

    1 can (2.8 ounces) french-fried onions, crushed
    1 jar (2 ounces) crumbled bacon *or* 3/4 cup cooked crumbled bacon
1/2 cup mayonnaise
    3 cups (12 ounces) shredded Swiss cheese
    1 jar (14 ounces) pizza sauce
    1 loaf (16 ounces) snack rye bread

In a bowl, combine the onions, bacon, mayonnaise and Swiss cheese. Spread about 1 teaspoon of pizza sauce on each slice of bread. Top with about 1 tablespoon of the cheese mixture. Cover and freeze in a single layer for up to 2 months, or bake on an ungreased baking sheet at 350° for 12-14 minutes or until heated through and cheese is melted. **Yield:** 20 appetizers.

To use frozen appetizers: Place on an ungreased baking sheet. Bake at 350° for 14-16 minutes or until heated through and cheese is melted.

Wontons with Sweet-Sour Sauce

(Pictured below)

Korrin Grigg, Neenah, Wisconsin

This super-simple finger food makes an awesome appetizer and is perfect for potlucks. I serve these crispy pork rolls with sweet-sour sauce, and they disappear in a hurry—folks can't seem to get enough of them.

    1 can (14 ounces) pineapple tidbits
    1/2 cup packed brown sugar
    1 tablespoon cornstarch
    1/3 cup cider vinegar
    1 tablespoon soy sauce
    1/2 cup chopped green pepper
    1/2 pound ground pork
    2 cups finely shredded cabbage
    3/4 cup finely chopped canned bean sprouts
    1 small onion, finely chopped
    2 eggs, lightly beaten
    1/2 teaspoon salt
    1/4 teaspoon pepper
    2 packages (12 ounces *each*) wonton wrappers*
Oil for frying

Drain pineapple, reserving juice. Set pineapple aside. In a saucepan, combine brown sugar and cornstarch; gradually stir in pineapple juice, vinegar and soy sauce until smooth. Bring to a boil; cook and stir for 2 minutes or until thickened. Reduce heat; stir in green pepper and pineapple. Cover and simmer for 5 minutes; set aside and keep warm.

In a bowl, combine pork, cabbage, sprouts, onion, eggs, salt and pepper. Place about 1 tablespoonful in the center of each wrapper. Moisten edges with water; fold opposite corners together over filling and press to seal. In an electric skillet, heat 1 in. of oil to 375°. Fry wontons for 2-1/2 minutes or until golden brown, turning once. Drain on paper towels. Serve with sauce. **Yield:** about 8-1/2 dozen (2-1/2 cups sauce).

*Editor's Note: Fill wonton wrappers a few at a time, keeping others covered until ready to use.

Clam-Ups

(Pictured above)

Patricia Kile, Greentown, Pennsylvania

These convenient appetizers can be assembled ahead and frozen before baking.

    1 can (6-1/2 ounces) minced clams
    2 tablespoons diced onion
    5 tablespoons butter, *divided*
    3-1/2 teaspoons all-purpose flour
    1/2 teaspoon prepared horseradish
    1/4 teaspoon garlic powder
    1/4 teaspoon Worcestershire sauce
Dash salt
    9 slices bread, crusts removed
Paprika

Drain clams, reserving juice; set aside. In a skillet, saute onion in 1 tablespoon butter until tender. Stir in flour until blended. Gradually add horseradish, garlic powder, Worcestershire sauce, salt and reserved clam juice. Bring to a boil; cook and stir for 2 minutes or until thickened. Remove from heat; stir in clams.

Flatten bread with a rolling pin. Melt remaining butter; brush one side of each slice of bread. Spread with clam mixture; roll up. Brush with remaining butter; sprinkle with paprika. Cut rolls into thirds; place on a greased baking sheet. Bake at 425° for 5-8 minutes or until lightly browned. Serve warm. **Yield:** 27 appetizers.

Bacon Cheeseburger Balls

(Pictured below)

Cathy Lendvoy, Boharm, Saskatchewan

When I serve these, my husband and sons are often fooled into thinking we're having plain meatballs until they cut into the flavorful filling inside.

>   1 egg
>   1 envelope onion soup mix
>   1 pound ground beef
>   2 tablespoons all-purpose flour
>   2 tablespoons milk
>   1 cup (4 ounces) finely shredded cheddar cheese
>   4 bacon strips, cooked and crumbled
> **COATING:**
>   2 eggs
>   1 cup crushed saltines (about 30 crackers)
>   5 tablespoons vegetable oil

In a bowl, combine egg and soup mix. Crumble beef over mixture and mix well. Divide into 36 portions; set aside. In a bowl, combine the flour and milk until smooth. Add cheese and bacon; mix well. Shape cheese mixture into 36 balls. Shape one beef portion around each cheese ball.

In a shallow bowl, beat the eggs. Place cracker crumbs in another bowl. Dip meatballs into egg, then coat with crumbs. In a large skillet over medium heat, cook meatballs in oil for 10-12 minutes or until the meat is no longer pink and coating is golden brown. **Yield:** 3 dozen.

Marinated Chicken Wings

(Pictured above)

Janie Botting, Sultan, Washington

I've made these nicely flavored chicken wings many times for get-togethers. They cook in the slow cooker while I finish up other last-minute details. They're so moist and tender…I always get lots of compliments and many requests for the recipe.

>   20 whole chicken wings* (about 4 pounds)
>   2 cups soy sauce
>   1/2 cup white wine *or* chicken broth
>   1/2 cup vegetable oil
>   2 to 3 garlic cloves, minced
>   2 tablespoons sugar
>   2 teaspoons ground ginger

Cut chicken wings into three sections; discard wing tips. Place wings in a large resealable heavy-duty plastic bag or 13-in. x 9-in. x 2-in. baking dish. In a bowl, combine remaining ingredients; mix well. Pour half of the sauce over chicken; turn to coat. Seal or cover the chicken and remaining sauce; refrigerate overnight. Drain chicken, discarding the marinade.

Place chicken in a 5-qt. slow cooker; top with reserved sauce. Cover and cook on low for 3-1/2 to 4 hours or until chicken juices run clear. Transfer wings to a serving dish; discard cooking juices. **Yield:** 18-20 servings.

***Editor's Note:** 4 pounds of uncooked chicken wing sections may be substituted for the whole chicken wings. Omit the first step of the recipe.

Three-Meat Stromboli

(Pictured at right)

Lorelei Hull, Luling, Louisiana

I made this hearty bread for a golf outing my husband attended and received many compliments. Several men asked for the recipe, and they've told me they make it often. It makes a good appetizer or sandwich for lunch.

> 2 loaves (1 pound *each*) frozen bread dough, thawed
> 2 tablespoons Dijon mustard
> 1/2 cup grated Parmesan cheese, *divided*
> 4 ounces pastrami, finely chopped
> 4 ounces pepperoni, finely chopped
> 4 ounces salami, finely chopped
> 1 cup (4 ounces) shredded Swiss cheese
> 1 egg, beaten

Roll each loaf of bread into a 12-in. x 7-in. rectangle. Spread mustard to within 1 in. of edges. Sprinkle each with 2 tablespoons of Parmesan cheese. Combine pastrami, pepperoni, salami and Swiss cheese; sprinkle over dough. Top with the remaining Parmesan.

Brush edges of dough with egg. Roll up, jelly-roll style, beginning with a long side. Seal edge and ends. Place seam side down on a greased baking sheet; cut three slits in the top of each loaf. Bake at 350° for 35-40 minutes. Slice; serve warm. **Yield:** 2 loaves (12-16 servings each).

Cheesy Mushroom Appetizers

Kathi Bloomer, Noblesville, Indiana

My husband loves these appetizers. Sometimes I think he makes up work functions just so I make them and he can snack on them at his desk!

> 2 tubes (8 ounces *each*) refrigerated crescent rolls
> 2 packages (8 ounces *each*) cream cheese, softened
> 3 cans (4 ounces *each*) mushroom stems and pieces, drained and chopped
> 1-1/4 teaspoons garlic powder
> 1/2 teaspoon Cajun seasoning
> 1 egg
> 1 tablespoon water
> 2 tablespoons grated Parmesan cheese

Unroll the crescent dough into two long rectangles; seal seams and perforations. In a mixing bowl, combine the cream cheese, mushrooms, garlic powder and Cajun seasoning. Spread over the dough to within 1 in. of the edges.

Roll up each rectangle, jelly-roll style, starting with a long side; seal edges. Place seam side down on a greased baking sheet. Beat egg and water; brush over dough. Sprinkle with cheese. Bake at 375° for 20-25 minutes or until golden brown. Cut into slices. **Yield:** 16 appetizers.

Taco Tater Skins

Phyllis Douglas, Fairview, Michigan

The idea for my recipe started with a food demonstration I didn't like. That version used things most people don't have on hand. So I decided to experiment, and out came Taco Tater Skins. They're great for parties as appetizers.

> 6 large russet potatoes
> 1/2 cup butter, melted
> 2 tablespoons taco seasoning
> 1 cup (4 ounces) shredded cheddar cheese
> 15 bacon strips, cooked and crumbled
> 3 green onions, chopped
> Salsa *and/or* sour cream, optional

Bake potatoes at 375° for 1 hour or until tender. Reduce heat to 350°. When cool enough to handle, cut the potatoes lengthwise into quarters. Scoop out pulp, leaving a 1/4-in. shell (save pulp for another use).

Combine the butter and taco seasoning; brush over both sides of potato skins. Place skin side down on a greased baking sheet. Sprinkle with cheese, bacon and onions. Bake for 5-10 minutes or until the cheese is melted. Serve with salsa and/or sour cream if desired. **Yield:** 2 dozen.

Skinny on Potatoes

Cooking a potato in its skin will retain most of its nutrients. This is true whether you bake or boil the spud. If you're using potatoes with the skin on, use a vegetable brush to scrub them well before cooking.

Savory Bread Strips

Mary Nichols, Dover, New Hampshire

For a friend's surprise party, I decided to try a new recipe and came up with this crispy bread topped with ham, olives and more. The savory ingredients in this irresistible appetizer blend so well that I'm always asked for the recipe.

1 package (1/4 ounce) active dry yeast
6-1/2 teaspoons sugar, *divided*
1/2 cup warm water (110° to 115°)
3 tablespoons olive oil
2 tablespoons dried minced onion
2 teaspoons dried basil
1 teaspoon dried oregano
1 teaspoon rubbed sage
1 teaspoon garlic powder
1/2 cup cold water
3 cups all-purpose flour
TOPPING:
1-1/2 cups chopped fully cooked ham
1 cup shredded Parmesan cheese
1/2 cup chopped ripe olives
1/2 cup chopped onion
1/2 cup minced fresh parsley
1/4 cup olive oil
2 garlic cloves, minced

Dissolve yeast and 1/2 teaspoon sugar in warm water; set aside. In a saucepan, combine oil, onion, basil, oregano, sage and garlic powder; cook over medium heat for 1 minute. Remove from the heat; stir in cold water. In a mixing bowl, combine flour and remaining sugar. Stir in oil and yeast mixtures.

Turn onto a lightly floured surface; knead for 3 minutes. Place dough on a greased 15-in. x 10-in. x 1-in. baking pan. Cover and let stand for 15 minutes. Pat dough evenly into pan. Combine topping ingredients; sprinkle over dough. Bake at 375° for 25-30 minutes or until well browned. Cut into 2-in. x 1-in. strips. **Yield:** about 6 dozen.

Bacon-Cheese Appetizer Pie

(Pictured below)

Joanie Elbourn, Gardner, Massachusetts

I first made this for an open house years ago and everybody liked it. It's very easy to make and tastes delicious. Cheesecake is popular in these parts—it's fun to have it for an appetizer instead of dessert for a change.

Pastry for a single-crust pie
3 packages (8 ounces *each*) cream cheese, softened
4 eggs, lightly beaten
1/4 cup milk
1 cup (4 ounces) shredded Swiss cheese
1/2 cup sliced green onions
6 bacon strips, cooked and crumbled
1/2 teaspoon salt
1/8 teaspoon pepper
1/8 teaspoon cayenne pepper

Roll the pastry into a 13-1/2-in. circle. Fit into the bottom and up the sides of an ungreased 9-in. springform pan. Lightly prick the bottom. Bake at 450° for 8-10 minutes or until lightly browned. Cool slightly.

In a mixing bowl, beat cream cheese until fluffy. Add eggs and milk; beat until smooth. Add cheese, onions, bacon, salt, pepper and cayenne; mix well. Pour into the crust. Bake at 350° for 40-45 minutes or until a knife inserted near the center comes out clean. Cool 20 minutes. Remove sides of pan. Cut into thin slices; serve warm. **Yield:** 16-20 appetizer servings.

Best of Country Appetizers/Hot Appetizers

Chicken Nut Puffs

(Pictured above)

Jo Groth, Plainfield, Iowa

Of the 15 to 20 appetizers I set out each year when hosting holiday parties, these savory meat puffs are the first to get snapped up by friends and family alike. People enjoy the zippy flavor. They're a nice finger food to eat since they're not sticky or drippy.

- 1-1/2 cups finely chopped cooked chicken
- 1/3 cup chopped almonds, toasted
- 1 cup chicken broth
- 1/2 cup vegetable oil
- 2 teaspoons Worcestershire sauce
- 1 tablespoon dried parsley flakes
- 1 teaspoon seasoned salt
- 1/2 to 1 teaspoon celery seed
- 1/8 teaspoon cayenne pepper
- 1 cup all-purpose flour
- 4 eggs

Combine the chicken and almonds; set aside. In a large saucepan, combine the broth, oil, Worcestershire sauce, parsley, salt, celery seed and pepper; bring to a boil. Add flour all at once; stir until a smooth ball forms. Remove from the heat; let stand for 5 minutes.

Add eggs, one at a time, beating well after each. Beat until smooth. Stir in chicken and almonds. Drop by heaping teaspoonfuls onto greased baking sheets. Bake at 450° for 12-14 minutes or until golden brown. Serve warm. **Yield:** about 6 dozen.

Cheesy Sausage Nachos

(Pictured at right)

Jane Sodergren, Red Wing, Minnesota

These flavorful nachos are very versatile. They are so hearty that I've served them as an entree, but also as an appealing appetizer. They get rave reviews either way.

- 3/4 pound bulk pork sausage
- 1/4 cup chopped onion
- 3 cups diced fresh tomatoes, *divided*
- 3/4 cup picante sauce
- 4 cups tortilla chips
- 3 cups (12 ounces) shredded Monterey Jack cheese, *divided*
- 1 medium ripe avocado, diced

In a skillet, cook sausage and onion over medium heat until meat is no longer pink; drain well. Add 2 cups tomatoes and picante sauce. Bring to a boil. Reduce heat; simmer, uncovered, for 20 minutes or until most of the liquid has evaporated.

Sprinkle tortilla chips over a 12-in. pizza pan. Top with 2 cups cheese and the sausage mixture; sprinkle with remaining cheese. Bake at 350° for 8-10 minutes or until cheese is melted. Sprinkle with avocado and remaining tomatoes. **Yield:** 8-10 servings.

Curried Olive Canapes

Robert Ulis, Alexandria, Virginia

These canapes are fast to assemble—you can make them in advance and heat them up at the last minute. We think they taste just as good with fat-free mayonnaise.

- 1-1/2 cups (6 ounces) shredded cheddar cheese
- 1 cup sliced ripe olives
- 1/2 cup mayonnaise
- 1/4 cup sliced green onions
- 1/2 teaspoon curry powder
- 1/4 to 1/2 teaspoon salt
- 3 English muffins, split

In a bowl, combine the first six ingredients and mix well. Spread over English muffins. Cut into quarters. Place on an ungreased baking sheet. Broil 4 in. from the heat for 1-2 minutes or until cheese is melted. Serve warm. **Yield:** 2 dozen.

Taco Meatball Ring

(Pictured at right)

Brenda Johnson, Davison, Michigan

While it looks complicated, this attractive meatball-filled ring is really very easy to assemble. My family loves tacos, and we find that the crescent roll dough is a nice change from the usual tortilla shells or chips. There are never any leftovers whether I serve this as a party appetizer or at a meal!

    2 cups (8 ounces) shredded cheddar cheese,
      divided
    2 tablespoons water
    2 to 4 tablespoons taco seasoning
    1/2 pound ground beef
    2 tubes (8 ounces *each*) refrigerated crescent rolls
    1/2 head iceberg lettuce, shredded
    1 medium tomato, chopped
    4 green onions, sliced
    1/2 cup sliced ripe olives
Sour cream
    2 small jalapeno peppers, seeded and sliced*
Salsa, optional

In a bowl, combine 1 cup cheese, water and taco seasoning. Add beef and mix well. Shape into 16 balls. Place 1 in. apart in an ungreased 15-in. x 10-in. x 1-in. baking pan. Bake, uncovered, at 400° for 12 minutes or until meat is no longer pink. Drain meatballs on paper towels. Reduce heat to 375°.

Arrange the crescent rolls on a greased 15-in. pizza pan, forming a ring with pointed ends facing the outer edge of the pan and the wide ends overlapping. Place a meatball on each roll; fold point over the meatball and tuck under wide end of roll (meatballs will be visible). Bake for 15-20 minutes or until rolls are golden brown.

Fill the center of ring with lettuce, tomato, onions, olives, remaining cheese, sour cream, jalapenos and salsa if desired. **Yield:** 8 servings.

*****Editor's Note:** When cutting or seeding hot peppers, use rubber or plastic gloves to protect your hands. Avoid touching your face.

Bell Pepper Nachos

(Pictured below left)

Aneta Kish, La Crosse, Wisconsin

Instead of tortilla chips, pepper pieces hold a savory cheese and rice topping in this colorful appetizer. Our family really digs into a plate of these nachos.

    2 medium green peppers
    1 medium sweet red pepper
    1 medium sweet yellow pepper
    2 medium plum tomatoes, seeded and chopped
    1/3 cup finely chopped onion
    1 teaspoon chili powder
    1/2 teaspoon ground cumin
  1-1/2 cups cooked rice
    1/2 cup shredded Monterey Jack cheese
    1/4 cup minced fresh cilantro
    1/4 teaspoon hot pepper sauce
    1/2 cup shredded sharp cheddar cheese

Cut peppers into 1-1/2- to 2-in. squares. Cut each square in half diagonally to form two triangles; set aside. In a lightly greased skillet, cook the tomatoes, onion, chili powder and cumin over medium heat for 3 minutes or until onion is tender, stirring occasionally. Remove from the heat. Add rice, Monterey Jack cheese, cilantro and hot pepper sauce; stir well.

Spoon a heaping tablespoon onto each pepper triangle. Place on greased baking sheets. Sprinkle with cheddar cheese. Broil 6-8 in. from the heat for 3-4 minutes or until cheese is bubbly and rice is heated through. **Yield:** 3-1/2 dozen.

Editor's Note: These appetizers can be assembled ahead of time. Place on baking sheets, cover and refrigerate for up to 8 hours before broiling.

Apple Sausage Appetizers

Dolores Barnas, Blasdell, New York

✓ Uses less fat, sugar or salt. Includes Nutritional Analysis and Diabetic Exchanges.

This no-fuss appetizer makes plenty, so it's great for a football party or holiday gathering…just serve with toothpicks.

- 2 jars (23 ounces *each*) unsweetened chunky applesauce
- 1/2 cup packed brown sugar
- 2 pounds fully cooked kielbasa *or* Polish sausage, cut into 1/2-inch slices
- 1 medium onion, chopped

In a bowl, combine applesauce and brown sugar. Stir in sausage and onion. Transfer to a greased 13-in. x 9-in. x 2-in. baking dish. Bake, uncovered, at 350° for 40-45 minutes or until bubbly. **Yield:** 20 servings.

Nutritional Analysis: One 1/2-cup serving (prepared with reduced-fat turkey Polish sausage) equals 117 calories, 404 mg sodium, 30 mg cholesterol, 14 g carbohydrate, 7 g protein, 4 g fat, 1 g fiber. **Diabetic Exchanges:** 1 fruit, 1 lean meat.

Tater Nuggets

Shelley Mitchell, Baldur, Manitoba

We enjoy snacking on these homemade tater treats after a long day of hard work on our farm. The addition of ham and cheese is a pleasant surprise.

- 2 cups hot mashed potatoes (without added milk or butter)
- 1 cup ground fully cooked ham
- 1 cup (4 ounces) shredded cheddar cheese
- 1/4 cup mayonnaise

- 2 eggs, beaten
- 1/4 cup finely chopped onion
- 1 teaspoon prepared mustard
- 1/2 teaspoon salt
- 1/4 teaspoon pepper
- 1-1/2 cups crushed cornflakes

Combine potatoes, ham, cheese, mayonnaise, eggs, onion, mustard, salt and pepper; shape into 1-in. balls. Roll in cornflakes. Place on greased baking sheets. Bake at 350° for 15 minutes or until golden brown. Serve warm. **Yield:** about 4 dozen.

Mini Chicken Turnovers

(Pictured below left)

Mary Detweiler, West Farmington, Ohio

I've been making these hearty tiny turnovers for several years. They take a little extra time to assemble, but it's worth it since they taste so special.

FILLING:
- 3 tablespoons chopped onion
- 3 tablespoons butter
- 1-3/4 cups shredded cooked chicken
- 3 tablespoons chicken broth
- 1/4 teaspoon *each* garlic salt, poultry seasoning and pepper
- 1 package (3 ounces) cream cheese, cubed

PASTRY:
- 1-1/2 cups all-purpose flour
- 1/2 teaspoon salt
- 1/2 teaspoon paprika
- 1/2 cup cold butter
- 4 to 5 tablespoons cold water

In a large skillet, saute onion in butter until tender. Stir in chicken, broth, seasonings and cream cheese; set aside. In a bowl, combine flour, salt and paprika; cut in butter until mixture resembles coarse crumbs. Gradually add water, tossing with a fork until a ball forms.

On a floured surface, roll out pastry to 1/16-in. thickness. Cut with a 2-1/2-in. round cookie cutter. Reroll scraps and cut more circles. Mound a heaping teaspoon of filling on half of each circle. Moisten edges with water; fold pastry over filling and press edges with a fork to seal.

Place on ungreased baking sheets. Repeat with remaining pastry and filling. Prick tops with a fork. Bake at 375° for 15-20 minutes or until golden brown. **Yield:** about 2-1/2 dozen.

Editor's Note: Turnovers can be baked, frozen and reheated at 375° for 5-7 minutes.

Seeding Peppers

Wash bell peppers before seeding. Cut in half by slicing vertically from one side of the stem all the way around to the other side of the stem. Break halves apart, and the seed core should pop right out.

Sausage-Stuffed Loaf

(Pictured below)

Suzanne Hansen, Arlington Heights, Illinois

This cheese-, spinach- and sausage-filled bread is a real crowd-pleaser. Tasty slices are great as a snack, served with a bowl of soup or as a fun appetizer at your next pizza party.

- 2 loaves (1 pound *each*) frozen bread dough
- 1 pound bulk Italian sausage
- 1 package (10 ounces) frozen chopped spinach, thawed and squeezed dry
- 4 cups (1 pound) shredded mozzarella cheese
- 1/4 cup grated Parmesan cheese
- 1 teaspoon dried oregano
- 1/2 teaspoon garlic powder
- 2 tablespoons butter, cubed
- 1 egg, lightly beaten

Thaw bread dough on a greased baking sheet according to package directions; let rise until doubled. Meanwhile, in a skillet over medium heat, cook the sausage until no longer pink. Drain and place in a bowl. Add spinach, cheeses, oregano and garlic powder; set aside. Roll each loaf of bread into a 14-in. x 12-in. rectangle. Spread sausage mixture lengthwise down the center of each rectangle. Gently press the filling down; dot with butter.

Bring edges of dough to the center over filling; pinch to seal. Return to the baking sheet, placing seam side down; tuck ends under and form into a crescent shape. Brush with egg. Bake at 350° for 20-25 minutes or until golden brown. Let stand for 5-10 minutes before cutting. Cool remaining loaf on a wire rack; wrap in foil and freeze for up to 3 months. **Yield:** 2 loaves.

To use frozen loaf: Thaw at room temperature for 2 hours. Unwrap and place on a greased baking sheet. Bake at 350° for 15-20 minutes or until heated through.

Pepper Poppers

(Pictured above)

Lisa Byington, Port Crane, New York

These creamy and zippy stuffed jalapenos may be the most popular treats I make. My husband is always hinting that I should prepare another batch.

- 1 package (8 ounces) cream cheese, softened
- 1 cup (4 ounces) shredded sharp cheddar cheese
- 1 cup (4 ounces) shredded Monterey Jack cheese
- 6 bacon strips, cooked and crumbled
- 1/4 teaspoon salt
- 1/4 teaspoon chili powder
- 1/4 teaspoon garlic powder
- 1 pound fresh jalapenos, halved lengthwise and seeded*
- 1/2 cup dry bread crumbs

Sour cream, onion dip *or* ranch salad dressing

In a mixing bowl, combine the cheeses, bacon and seasonings; mix well. Spoon about 2 tablespoonfuls into each pepper half. Roll in bread crumbs. Place in a greased 15-in. x 10-in. x 1-in. baking pan. Bake, uncovered, at 300° for 20 minutes for spicy flavor, 30 minutes for medium and 40 minutes for mild. Serve with sour cream, dip or dressing. **Yield:** about 2 dozen.

*Editor's Note: When cutting or seeding hot peppers, use rubber or plastic gloves to protect your hands. Avoid touching your face.

Party Franks

(Pictured at right)

Lucille Howell, Portland, Oregon

These tiny tangy appetizers have such broad appeal. I prepare them often for holiday gatherings, weddings and family reunions. They're convenient to serve at parties since the sauce can be made ahead, then just reheated with the franks before serving.

        3/4 cup chopped onion
        2 tablespoons vegetable oil
        1 cup ketchup
        1/2 cup water
        1/2 cup cider vinegar
        2 tablespoons sugar
        2 tablespoons Worcestershire sauce
        2 tablespoons honey
        2 teaspoons ground mustard
        2 teaspoons paprika
        3/4 teaspoon salt
        1/4 teaspoon pepper
        1/8 teaspoon hot pepper sauce
        1 large lemon, sliced
    2-1/2 to 3 pounds miniature hot dogs *or* smoked
        sausage links

In a saucepan, saute onion in oil until tender. Stir in the next 11 ingredients. Add lemon. Bring to a boil. Reduce heat; simmer, uncovered, for 20-25 minutes or until slightly thickened, stirring occasionally. Discard lemon slices.

Place hot dogs in a 13-in. x 9-in. x 2-in. baking dish. Top with sauce. Bake, uncovered, at 350° for 18-20 minutes or until heated through. Keep warm; serve with toothpicks. **Yield:** 25-30 servings.

Bacon-Wrapped Water Chestnuts

Midge Scurlock, Creston, Iowa

My husband, Ray, and I do lots of entertaining. We always start off with appetizers like these tempting morsels. This party dish is easy to prepare and appealing to serve. Our friends love it.

        8 bacon strips
        2 cans (8 ounces *each*) whole water chestnuts,
            drained
        3/4 cup ketchup
        1 jar (2-1/2 ounces) strained peach baby food
        1/4 cup sugar
    Dash salt

Cut bacon strips in half lengthwise and then in half widthwise. Wrap each bacon piece around a water chestnut; secure with a toothpick. Place in an ungreased 13-in. x 9-in. x 2-in. baking dish. Bake, uncovered, at 350° for 25 minutes, turning once; drain if necessary.

In a small bowl, combine all of the remaining ingredients. Drizzle over water chestnuts. Bake 25-35 minutes longer or until the bacon is crisp. Serve warm. **Yield:** 32 appetizers.

Tomato Leek Tarts

Kathleen Tribble, Santa Ynez, California

These attractive tarts are a scrumptious snack for two people. The crisp pastry crust cuts easily into wedges.

        1 package (15 ounces) refrigerated pie pastry
        1 cup (4 ounces) shredded provolone cheese
        1 pound leeks (white portion only), sliced
        6 medium plum tomatoes, thinly sliced
        1/4 cup grated Parmesan cheese
    1-1/2 teaspoons garlic powder
        1/8 teaspoon pepper
        1 cup (8 ounces) shredded mozzarella cheese

Place both pastry sheets on greased baking sheets. Sprinkle each with provolone cheese, leaving 1 in. around edges. Arrange leeks and tomato slices over provolone cheese. Sprinkle with Parmesan cheese, garlic powder and pepper. Top with mozzarella. Fold edges over filling.

Bake at 425° for 18-22 minutes or until crusts are lightly browned. Cut into wedges. Serve warm. **Yield:** 2 tarts.

Party Planner

An appetizer buffet is a fun twist on entertaining and lends itself to a less formal atmosphere than a traditional sit-down dinner. But don't be intimidated by such an undertaking...these helpful hints will make it a snap.

For an appetizer buffet that serves as the meal, offer five or six different appetizers and plan on eight to nine pieces per guest. If you'll also be serving a meal, two to three pieces per person is sufficient.

In order to appeal to everyone's tastes and diets, have a balance of hearty and low-calorie appetizers as well as hot and cold choices.

So that you can spend more time with guests, look for appetizers that can be made ahead and require little last-minute fuss.

Reuben Roll-Ups

(Pictured above)

Patty Kile, Greentown, Pennsylvania

This recipe turns the popular Reuben sandwich into an interesting and hearty snack. We love these roll-ups at our house.

- 1 tube (10 ounces) refrigerated pizza dough
- 1 cup sauerkraut, well drained
- 1 tablespoon Thousand Island salad dressing
- 4 slices corned beef, halved
- 4 slices Swiss cheese, halved

Roll dough into a 12-in. x 9-in. rectangle. Cut into eight 3-in. x 4-1/2-in. rectangles. Combine sauerkraut and salad dressing. Place a slice of beef on each rectangle. Top with about 2 tablespoons of the sauerkraut mixture and a slice of cheese. Roll up. Place with seam side down on a greased baking sheet. Bake at 425° for 12-14 minutes or until golden. **Yield:** 8 roll-ups.

Pork Egg Rolls

Jody Minke, Forest Lake, Minnesota

I take these hearty egg rolls and their tasty sweet and sour sauce to every family gathering.

- 1/2 pound ground pork
- 3/4 cup shredded cabbage
- 1/2 cup chopped celery
- 4 green onions, sliced
- 3 tablespoons vegetable oil
- 1/2 cup salad shrimp, chopped
- 1/2 cup water chestnuts, chopped
- 1/2 cup bean sprouts, chopped
- 1 garlic clove, minced
- 2 to 3 tablespoons soy sauce
- 1 teaspoon sugar
- 8 refrigerated egg roll wrappers*
- Oil for frying

SWEET 'N' SOUR SAUCE:
- 1 cup sugar
- 2 tablespoons cornstarch
- 1 teaspoon seasoned salt
- 1/2 cup white vinegar
- 1/2 cup water
- 1 tablespoon maraschino cherry juice, optional
- 1 teaspoon Worcestershire sauce

In a large skillet, cook pork over medium heat until no longer pink; drain. Remove pork with a slotted spoon and set aside. In the same skillet, stir-fry cabbage, celery and onions in oil until crisp-tender. Add shrimp, water chestnuts, bean sprouts, garlic, soy sauce, sugar and reserved pork; stir-fry 4 minutes longer or until liquid has evaporated. Remove from the heat.

Position egg roll wrappers with a corner facing you. Spoon 1/3 cup pork mixture on the bottom third of each wrapper. Fold a bottom corner over filling; fold sides over filling toward center. Moisten top corner with water; roll up tightly to seal. In an electric skillet, heat 1 in. of oil to 375°. Fry egg rolls for 1-2 minutes on each side or until golden brown. Drain on paper towels.

For sauce, combine the sugar, cornstarch and seasoned salt in a saucepan; gradually add the remaining ingredients. Bring to a boil; cook and stir for 2 minutes or until thickened. Serve with egg rolls. **Yield:** 8 egg rolls.

***Editor's Note:** Fill egg roll wrappers one at a time, keeping the others covered until ready to use.

Simmered Smoked Links

Maxine Cenker, Weirton, West Virginia

A tasty sweet-sour sauce glazes bite-size sausages in this recipe. Serve these effortless appetizers with toothpicks at parties or holiday get-togethers.

> 2 packages (16 ounces *each*) miniature smoked sausage links
> 1 cup packed brown sugar
> 1/2 cup ketchup
> 1/4 cup prepared horseradish

Place sausages in a slow cooker. Combine brown sugar, ketchup and horseradish; pour over sausages. Cover and cook on low for 4 hours. **Yield:** 16-20 servings.

Salsa Strips

(Pictured below)

Joann Woloszyn, Fredonia, New York

I rely on refrigerated crescent rolls to make these crisp Southwestern appetizers. Choose mild, medium or hot salsa to suit your taste.

> 1 tube (8 ounces) refrigerated crescent rolls
> 2 tablespoons Dijon mustard
> 3/4 cup salsa
> 1 cup (4 ounces) shredded mozzarella cheese
> Minced fresh cilantro

Unroll crescent roll dough and separate into four rectangles. Place on greased baking sheets. Spread mustard and salsa on each rectangle. Bake at 350° for 10 minutes. Sprinkle with cheese; bake 8-10 minutes longer or until golden brown. Cool for 10 minutes. Cut each into four strips; sprinkle with cilantro. **Yield:** 16 appetizers.

Ham 'n' Cheese Tortillas

(Pictured above)

Jamie Whitaker, Aurora, Missouri

My family eats these tasty tortillas as fast as I can make them. Good thing they can be made in a hurry! They're a new and flavorful way to serve ham and cheese.

> Vegetable oil for frying
> 6 flour tortillas (10 inches), quartered
> 3 packages (6 ounces *each*) boiled ham (24 slices)
> 4-1/2 cups shredded cheddar cheese
> 1 cup picante sauce *or* salsa
> Garlic salt
> Sour cream and minced chives, optional

In an electric skillet, heat 2 in. of oil to 375°. Fry tortilla wedges, a few at a time, until lightly browned and crispy. Drain on paper towels. Place wedges in a single layer on baking sheets.

Top each with a folded ham slice, 3 tablespoons cheese and 2 teaspoons picante sauce. Sprinkle with garlic salt. Broil 4-6 in. from the heat until cheese is melted, about 2 minutes. Serve warm. If desired, top with a dollop of sour cream and sprinkle with chives. **Yield:** 2 dozen.

Salsa Suggestion

Numerous kinds of salsa are available in supermarkets, ranging from mild to hot. Stir several teaspoons of your favorite salsa into plain yogurt or sour cream for an almost-instant dip for chips.

Stuffed Turkey Spirals

(Pictured above)

Renee Aupperle, Litiz, Pennsylvania

To create these impressive appetizers, I roll up turkey breast halves with ham and cheese, bake and slice them, then serve them with a creamy basil sauce. They're great for a buffet because you can prepare them ahead and bake them right before serving.

        2 boneless skinless turkey breast halves
            (1 pound *each*)
    1/4 cup olive oil, *divided*
        4 teaspoons dried basil, *divided*
        1 pound thinly sliced deli ham
        1 pound thinly sliced Swiss cheese
        1 teaspoon salt
        1 teaspoon pepper
BASIL SAUCE:
        2 cups mayonnaise
    1/2 cup milk
        1 to 2 tablespoons dried basil
        1 teaspoon sugar

Cut each turkey breast horizontally from long side to within 1/2 in. of opposite side. Open flat; cover with plastic wrap. Flatten into 10-in. x 1/2-in. rectangles. Remove plastic; top each with 1 teaspoon oil and 1 teaspoon basil. Layer with ham and cheese to within 1 in. of edges. Roll up jelly-roll style, starting with a long side; tie with kitchen string. Place on a rack in a roasting pan.

In a small bowl, combine salt, pepper and remaining oil and basil; spoon some over turkey. Bake at 325° for 75-90 minutes or until a meat thermometer reads 170°, basting occasionally with remaining oil mixture.

In a blender or food processor, combine the sauce ingredients; cover and process until blended. Cool turkey

for 5 minutes before slicing; serve with basil sauce. **Yield:** about 30 servings.

Onion Brie Appetizers

(Pictured below)

Carole Resnick, Cleveland, Ohio

Guests will think you spent hours preparing these appetizers, but they're really easy to assemble. The combination of Brie, caramelized onions and caraway is terrific.

        2 medium onions, thinly sliced
        3 tablespoons butter
        2 tablespoons brown sugar
    1/2 teaspoon white wine vinegar
        1 sheet frozen puff pastry, thawed
        4 ounces Brie *or* Camembert, rind removed, softened
        1 to 2 teaspoons caraway seeds
        1 egg
        2 teaspoons water

In a large skillet, cook the onions, butter, brown sugar and vinegar over medium-low heat until onions are golden brown, stirring frequently. Remove with a slotted spoon; cool to room temperature.

On a lightly floured surface, roll puff pastry into an 11-in. x 8-in. rectangle. Spread Brie over pastry. Cover with the onions; sprinkle with caraway seeds. Roll up one long side to the middle of the dough; roll up the other side so the two rolls meet in the center. Using a serrated knife, cut into 1/2-in. slices. Place on parchment paper-lined baking sheets; flatten to 1/4-in. thickness. Refrigerate for 15 minutes.

In a small bowl, beat egg and water; brush over slices. Bake at 375° for 12-14 minutes or until puffed and golden brown. Serve warm. **Yield:** 1-1/2 dozen.

Southwestern Onion Rings

(Pictured above)

Tamra Kriedeman, Enderlin, North Dakota

These light crispy onion rings are sliced thin and spiced just right with garlic powder, cayenne pepper, chili powder and cumin. My family loves them!

        2 large sweet onions
    2-1/2 cups buttermilk
        2 eggs
        3 tablespoons water
    1-3/4 cups all-purpose flour
        2 teaspoons salt
        2 teaspoons chili powder
        1 to 2 teaspoons cayenne pepper
        1 teaspoon sugar
        1 teaspoon garlic powder
        1 teaspoon ground cumin
    Oil for deep-fat frying

Cut onions into 1/4-in. slices; separate into rings. Place in a bowl; cover with buttermilk and soak for 30 minutes, stirring twice. In another bowl, beat eggs and water. In a shallow dish, combine the flour, salt, chili powder, cayenne, sugar, garlic powder and cumin. Drain onion rings; dip in egg mixture, then coat with flour mixture.

In an electric skillet or deep-fat fryer, heat 1 in. of oil to 375°. Fry onion rings, a few at a time, for 1 to 1-1/2 minutes on each side or until golden brown. Drain on paper towels. **Yield:** 8 servings.

Sweet-Sour Sausage Bites

Maretta Bullock, McNeil, Arkansas

As a pastor's wife, I frequently entertain church groups in my home, so I'm always looking for new recipes. These quick and easy appetizers are not only delicious, they're colorful, too. I've made them many times.

    1/2 pound fully cooked smoked sausage, cut into
            1/2-inch slices
        1 can (20 ounces) pineapple chunks
        4 teaspoons cornstarch
    1/2 teaspoon salt
    1/2 cup maple syrup
    1/3 cup water
    1/3 cup white vinegar
        1 large green pepper, cut into 3/4-inch pieces
    1/2 cup maraschino cherries

In a large skillet, saute the sausage for 3-5 minutes or until lightly browned. Drain sausage on paper towels; set aside. Drain pineapple, reserving juice; set the pineapple aside.

In a large skillet, combine the cornstarch, salt and reserved pineapple juice until smooth. Stir in the maple syrup, water and vinegar. Bring to a boil; cook and stir for 2-3 minutes or until thickened. Add the sausage, green pepper, cherries and pineapple. Simmer, uncovered, for 5 minutes or until the peppers are crisp-tender. Transfer to a shallow serving dish. Serve with toothpicks. **Yield:** 4 cups.

RANCH SNACK MIX

POPCORN NUT CRUNCH

CHEESE BALL SNACK MIX

SPICY PARTY MIX

SEASONED SNACK MIX

CALIFORNIA FRIED WALNUTS

SNACK MIXES & NUTS

Cayenne Pretzels

Gayle Zebo, Warren, Pennsylvania

These easy-to-coat, well-seasoned pretzels were a huge hit when I set them out in bowls at my daughter's graduation party a number of years ago. I've found that the longer they sit, the spicier they get!

- 1 cup vegetable oil
- 1 envelope ranch salad dressing mix
- 1 teaspoon garlic salt
- 1 teaspoon cayenne pepper
- 2 packages (10 ounces *each*) pretzel sticks

In a small bowl, combine the oil, dressing mix, garlic salt and cayenne. Divide pretzels between two ungreased 15-in. x 10-in. x 1-in. baking pans. Pour oil mixture over pretzels; stir to coat.

Bake at 200° for 1-1/4 to 1-1/2 hours or until the pretzels are golden brown, stirring occasionally. Cool completely. Store in an airtight container. **Yield:** 3-1/2 quarts.

Sugarcoated Spanish Peanuts

Judy Jungwirth, Athol, South Dakota

Once we start eating these sweet peanuts, it's hard to stop. We gobble them up by the handfuls, so it's good the recipe yields a big batch.

- 1-1/2 cups sugar
- 3/4 cup water
- 1 tablespoon maple flavoring
- 4-1/2 cups raw Spanish peanuts with skins
- 1/2 teaspoon salt

In a large saucepan, combine the sugar, water, maple flavoring and spanish peanuts. Cook and stir over medium heat for 20 minutes or until almost all of the liquid is absorbed. Spread into a greased 15-in. x 10-in. x 1-in. baking pan; sprinkle with salt.

Bake at 350° for 24-26 minutes or until peanuts are well coated, stirring two to three times. Remove to a waxed paper-lined baking sheet to cool completely. Store in an airtight container. **Yield:** 7 cups.

Happy Trails Snack Mix

(Pictured above)

Sharon Thompson, Oskaloosa, Iowa

Both salty and sweet, this colorful snack mix has an appealing assortment of pretzels, cereal, dried fruits and candies. It's yummy!

- 3 cups miniature pretzels
- 2 cups mixed nuts
- 1 cup Kix cereal
- 1 cup chopped dried apple
- 1 cup raisins
- 3/4 cup chopped dried pineapple
- 1 package (2.17 ounces) Skittles bite-size candies
- 1 package (1.69 ounces) milk chocolate M&M's

Combine all ingredients in a large bowl. Store in an airtight container. **Yield:** 2 quarts.

Roasted Mixed Nuts

Carolyn Zimmerman, Fairbury, Illinois

It's impossible to stop eating these savory nuts once you start. We love to munch on them as an evening snack.

- 1 pound mixed nuts
- 1/4 cup maple syrup
- 2 tablespoons brown sugar
- 1 envelope ranch salad dressing mix

In a bowl, combine the nuts and maple syrup; mix well. Sprinkle with brown sugar and salad dressing mix; stir gently to coat. Spread in a greased 15-in. x 10-in. x 1-in. baking pan. Bake at 300° for 20-25 minutes or until lightly browned. Cool completely. Store in an airtight container. **Yield:** 3 cups

Curried Cashews

Gertrude Wood, Ellicottville, New York

Curry powder is the key to these tasty cashews, which are perfect as a party snack or hostess gift. These unusual nuts were served at an open house I attended. I tracked down the recipe and now make them often for friends.

- 1/4 cup butter
- 1 can (10 ounces) salted cashews
- 2 tablespoons curry powder
- 1/2 teaspoon salt

In a skillet, melt butter. Add cashews; cook and stir over medium heat until lightly browned, about 10 minutes. Remove to paper towels to drain. Sprinkle with curry powder and salt. Cool completely. Store in an airtight container. **Yield:** 2 cups.

Cocoa Munch Mix

(Pictured at right)

Amanda Denton, Barre, Vermont

This sweet snack is a nice change of pace from the typical cookies and brownies found at bake sales. Packed in reseal-able bags, the mix always goes fast. It's great to take along on camping trips, too.

- 4 cups Cheerios
- 4 cups Chex cereal
- 1 cup slivered almonds
- 2 tablespoons baking cocoa
- 2 tablespoons sugar
- 1/2 cup butter, melted
- 1 cup raisins
- 1 package (12 ounces) vanilla *or* white chips

In a large bowl, combine the cereals and almonds. In a small bowl, combine cocoa, sugar and butter. Pour over cereal mixture and toss to coat. Pour into a greased 13-in. x 9-in. x 2-in. baking pan. Bake at 250° for 1 hour, stirring every 15 minutes. Cool completely. Stir in raisins and chips. Store in an airtight container. **Yield:** 10 servings.

Ranch Snack Mix

(Pictured below)

Linda Murphy, Pulaski, Wisconsin

This is a wonderful fast-to-fix munchie. The recipe makes a generous 24 cups and doesn't involve any cooking. It's a cinch to package in individual snack bags and keeps its crunch.

- 1 package (12 ounces) miniature pretzels
- 2 packages (6 ounces *each*) Bugles
- 1 can (10 ounces) salted cashews
- 1 package (6 ounces) bite-size cheddar cheese fish crackers
- 1 envelope ranch salad dressing mix
- 3/4 cup vegetable oil

In two large bowls, combine the pretzels, Bugles, cashews and crackers. Sprinkle with dressing mix; toss gently to combine. Drizzle with oil; toss until well coated. Store in airtight containers. **Yield:** 6 quarts.

Corny Snack Mix

Sandy Wehring, Fremont, Ohio

It's hard to stop munching this yummy snack mix! Melted vanilla chips make a delightful coating for the crisp corn chips, cereal and popcorn. This snack mix is quick and easy to toss together. I like to keep it on hand for when our five grandchildren visit.

- 3 quarts popped popcorn
- 1 package (15 ounces) Corn Pops cereal
- 1 package (15 ounces) corn chips
- 2 packages (10 to 12 ounces *each*) vanilla *or* white chips

In several large bowls, combine the popcorn, Corn Pops and corn chips. In a saucepan over medium-low heat, melt chips; stir until smooth. Pour over popcorn mixture and toss to coat. Spread in two 15-in. x 10-in. x 1-in. pans. Cool completely. Store in airtight containers. **Yield:** 7-1/2 quarts.

Seasoned Snack Mix

(Pictured above)

Flo Burtnett, Gage, Oklahoma

You'll never miss the oil or nuts in this well-seasoned party mix. I keep some on hand for whenever the munchies strike.

✓ **Uses less fat, sugar or salt. Includes Nutritional Analysis and Diabetic Exchanges.**

  3 cups Rice Chex cereal
  3 cups Corn Chex cereal
  3 cups Cheerios
  3 cups pretzels
  2 teaspoons Worcestershire sauce
  2 teaspoons butter-flavored sprinkles
1/2 teaspoon garlic powder
1/2 teaspoon seasoned salt
1/2 teaspoon onion powder

In a 15-in. x 10-in. x 1-in. baking pan, combine cereals and pretzels. Lightly coat with nonstick cooking spray; drizzle with Worcestershire sauce. Combine the remaining ingredients and sprinkle over cereal mixture.

Bake at 200° for 1-1/2 hours, stirring every 30 minutes. Cool completely. Store in an airtight container. **Yield:** 3 quarts.

Nutritional Analysis: One serving (1 cup) equals 115 calories, 1 g fat (trace saturated fat), 0 cholesterol, 400 mg sodium, 25 g carbohydrate, 1 g fiber, 3 g protein. **Diabetic Exchange:** 1-1/2 starch.

Oat Snack Mix

Patti Brandt, Reedsburg, Wisconsin

Kids of all ages seem to enjoy the creative combination of ingredients in this not-so-sweet mix. My three children would rather snack on this than on candy. I'm happy to make it for them since it's easy enough to put together and stores well in the pantry.

1/2 cup butter
1/3 cup honey
1/4 cup packed brown sugar
  1 teaspoon ground cinnamon
1/2 teaspoon salt
  3 cups square oat cereal
1-1/2 cups old-fashioned oats
  1 cup chopped walnuts
1/2 cup dried cranberries
1/2 cup chocolate-covered raisins

In a saucepan or microwave-safe bowl, combine the butter, honey, brown sugar, cinnamon and salt; heat until the butter is melted. Stir until the sugar is dissolved. In a large bowl, combine cereal, oats and nuts. Drizzle with butter mixture and mix well. Place in a greased 15-in. x 10-in. x 1-in. baking pan.

Bake, uncovered, at 275° for 45 minutes, stirring every 15 minutes. Cool for 15 minutes, stirring occasionally. Stir in cranberries and chocolate-covered raisins. Cool completely. Store in an airtight container. **Yield:** about 6 cups.

Popcorn Nut Crunch

(Pictured at right)

Midge Stolte, Blackfalds, Alberta

Our brood says it's not Christmas here until I make this snack mix. I usually double the recipe so I can put some in tins or baskets for hostess gifts.

> 2 quarts popped popcorn
> 1 cup blanched whole almonds, toasted
> 1 cup *each* pecan halves, cashews, Brazil nuts
> and hazelnuts, toasted
> 1-1/2 cups sugar
> 1 cup dark corn syrup
> 1/2 cup butter
> 1 teaspoon vanilla extract
> 1/2 teaspoon ground cinnamon

Place the popcorn and nuts in a lightly greased 5-qt. Dutch oven. Bake at 250° for 20 minutes. Meanwhile, in a medium saucepan, combine sugar, corn syrup and butter; bring to a boil over medium heat, stirring constantly. Cook, without stirring, until a candy thermometer reads 290° (soft-crack stage). Remove from the heat; stir in vanilla and cinnamon.

Pour a small amount at a time over popcorn mixture, stirring constantly until the mixture is well coated. Immediately spread on greased baking sheets. Cool completely; break into pieces. Store in airtight containers. **Yield:** about 4 quarts.

Fruit 'n' Nut Trail Mix

(Pictured below)

Pat Habiger, Spearville, Kansas

This snack recipe has a good mix of fruit and nuts. The mild cinnamon flavor adds a nice touch.

> 1/4 cup sunflower kernels
> 2 tablespoons butter
> 4 cups old-fashioned oats
> 1/2 cup vegetable oil

> 3/4 cup cashew halves
> 2/3 cup slivered almonds, toasted
> 1/2 cup sesame seeds, toasted
> 1/2 cup packed brown sugar
> 1/2 cup honey
> 1 teaspoon ground cinnamon
> 1-1/4 cups assorted bite-size dried fruit (raisins,
> apricots, dates, apples, bananas)

In a large skillet over medium heat, lightly toast sunflower kernels in butter; remove and set aside. In the same skillet, lightly toast oats in oil. Add the sunflower kernels, cashews, almonds and sesame seeds. Combine the brown sugar, honey and cinnamon; add to oat mixture. Cook and stir for 5 minutes.

Spread in two ungreased 15-in. x 10-in. x 1-in. baking pans. Bake at 350° for 15-20 minutes or until golden brown, stirring every 5 minutes. Cool, stirring occasionally. Stir in dried fruit. Store in an airtight container. **Yield:** 10 cups.

Italian Nut Medley

Karen Riordan, Fern Creek, Kentucky

Italian salad dressing mix is the easy secret ingredient—it adds just the right zip to plain mixed nuts.

> 2 tablespoons butter
> 4 cups mixed nuts
> 1 tablespoon soy sauce
> 1 envelope Italian salad dressing mix

In a skillet, melt the butter over medium heat. Add nuts; cook and stir constantly for 2 minutes. Stir in soy sauce. Sprinkle with salad dressing mix; stir to coat. Immediately transfer to a greased baking pan and spread in a single layer. Cool. Store in an airtight container. **Yield:** 4 cups.

Party-Time Popcorn

(Pictured above)

Darlene Smith, Brownsburg, Indiana

This fun snack mix combines crunchy peanuts and popcorn with a perky dill flavor, plus other seasonings. Once you start munching, you won't be able to stop!

    2 quarts popped popcorn
    3 cups shoestring potato sticks
    1 cup salted mixed nuts *or* peanuts
    1/4 cup butter, melted
    1 teaspoon dill weed
    1 teaspoon Worcestershire sauce
    1/2 teaspoon lemon-pepper seasoning
    1/4 teaspoon garlic powder
    1/4 teaspoon onion salt

In an ungreased roasting pan, combine the popcorn, potato sticks and nuts. Combine all of the the remaining ingredients; pour over popcorn mixture and toss to coat. Bake, uncovered, at 325° for 8-10 minutes, stirring once. Cool completely. Store in an airtight container. **Yield:** 2 quarts.

Sugar 'n' Spice Nuts

(Pictured on front cover)

Lori Brouwer, Cumberland, British Columbia

It just isn't Christmas until these crunchy munchers are in the oven. The wonderful aroma of ginger, cinnamon and nuts fills the kitchen with festivity when I bake this snack.

    2 egg whites
    4 teaspoons water
    3 cups walnut halves
    2 cups pecan halves
    1 cup whole unblanched almonds
    1 cup sugar
    1 tablespoon ground cinnamon
    1 teaspoon ground ginger
    1 teaspoon grated orange peel

    1/2 teaspoon salt
    1/2 teaspoon ground nutmeg
    1/2 teaspoon ground allspice
    1/4 teaspoon ground cloves

In a mixing bowl, beat egg whites and water until frothy. Add nuts; stir gently to coat. Combine all of the remaining ingredients. Add to nut mixture and stir gently to coat. Spread into two greased 15-in. x 10-in. x 1-in. baking pans.

Bake, uncovered, at 300° for 20-25 minutes or until lightly browned, stirring every 10 minutes. Cool completely. Store in an airtight container. **Yield:** 8 cups.

Spicy Party Mix

(Pictured below)

June Mullins, Livonia, Missouri

Sesame seeds are a fun addition in this savory snack mix. Both children and adults go for this crispy combo.

    10 cups Crispix cereal
     2 cups salted peanuts
    1-1/2 cups pretzel sticks
    1/2 cup sesame seeds, toasted
    1/2 cup vegetable oil
     2 tablespoons lemon juice
     1 tablespoon chili powder
     1 tablespoon curry powder
     1 teaspoon garlic salt
     1 teaspoon onion salt
    1/2 teaspoon ground cumin

In a large bowl, combine the cereal, peanuts, pretzels and sesame seeds. In a saucepan, combine the remaining ingredients; bring to a boil. Pour over the cereal mixture and stir to coat. Spread in a greased 15-in. x 10-in. x 1-in. baking pan.

Bake at 250° for 10 minutes or until golden brown, stirring once. Cool completely. Store in an airtight container. **Yield:** 4 quarts.

Popcorn Snack Mix

Heidi Harrington, Steuben, Maine

With steak sauce, curry and garlic powder, this snack mix has a bold, spicy taste.

        3 quarts popped popcorn
2-1/3 cups salted peanuts
        2 cups pretzel sticks
        2 cups miniature cheese crackers
    1/3 cup butter, melted
    3/4 teaspoon salt
    3/4 teaspoon *each* curry powder, garlic powder
            and onion powder
    3/4 teaspoon steak sauce

In a large bowl, combine popcorn, peanuts, pretzels and crackers. Combine remaining ingredients. Pour over popcorn mixture; toss to coat. Place in two ungreased 15-in. x 10-in. x 1-in. baking pans.

Bake, uncovered, at 250° for 1 hour; stir every 15 minutes. Cool completely. Store in an airtight container. **Yield:** about 4 quarts.

Oyster Cracker Snack

Verona Koehlmoos, Pilger, Nebraska

This is a quick-to-fix recipe I make often. Everyone eats these crackers by the handful!

✓ Uses less fat, sugar or salt. Includes Nutritional Analysis and Diabetic Exchanges.

    2 packages (10 ounces *each*) oyster crackers
    3/4 cup vegetable oil
        1 envelope ranch salad dressing mix
        1 teaspoon dill weed
    1/2 teaspoon onion powder
    1/2 teaspoon garlic powder
    1/2 teaspoon lemon-pepper seasoning

Place crackers in a large bowl. In a small bowl, combine the remaining ingredients; pour over crackers and mix well. Let stand for 2 hours. Store in an airtight container. **Yield:** 12 cups.

Nutritional Analysis: One serving (1/2 cup) equals 168 calories, 10 g fat (1 g saturated fat), 0 cholesterol, 411 mg sodium, 18 g carbohydrate, 1 g fiber, 2 g protein. **Diabetic Exchanges:** 2 fat, 1 starch.

Spicy Ribbon Potato Chips

(Pictured above right)

Sue Murphy, Greenwood, Michigan

You won't settle for store-bought chips again after trying these crispy deep-fried snacks. Seasoned with chili powder and cayenne pepper, the zippy paper-thin chips are surefire crowd-pleasers.

    4 medium unpeeled baking potatoes
    4 teaspoons salt, *divided*
    4 cups ice water
    1 tablespoon chili powder

        1 teaspoon garlic salt
    1/4 to 1/2 teaspoon cayenne pepper
Oil for deep-fat frying

Using a vegetable peeler or metal cheese slicer, cut potatoes into very thin lengthwise strips. Place in a large bowl; add 3 teaspoons salt and ice water. Soak for 30 minutes; drain. Place potatoes on paper towels and pat dry. In a bowl, combine the chili powder, garlic salt, cayenne and remaining salt; set aside.

In an electric skillet or deep-fat fryer, heat oil to 375°. Cook potatoes in oil in batches for 3-4 minutes or until deep golden brown, stirring frequently. Remove with a slotted spoon; drain on paper towels. Immediately sprinkle with seasoning mixture. Store in an airtight container. **Yield:** 6-8 servings.

A Kernel on Popcorn

To pop popcorn on the stove, use a 3- or 4-quart pan with a loose-fitting lid. Add 1/3 cup vegetable oil for every cup of kernels.

Heat the oil to between 400° and 460°. Drop in one kernel, and when it pops, add the rest—just enough to cover bottom of pan with a single layer.

Cover pan and shake to spread the oil. When popping begins to slow, remove pan from heat. The hot oil will continue to pop the remaining kernels.

Spiced Nut Mix

(Pictured above)

Patti Holland, Parker, Colorado

When we were newlyweds, our first Christmas was pretty lean. I usually make presents, but that year I had no idea what I could afford. A friend gave me this recipe and a sack of ingredients. I think of her every time I stir up this mix.

        3 egg whites
        2 teaspoons water
        2 cans (12 ounces *each*) salted peanuts
        1 cup whole blanched almonds
        1 cup walnut halves
    1-3/4 cups sugar
        3 tablespoons pumpkin pie spice
      3/4 teaspoon salt
        1 cup raisins

In a mixing bowl, beat egg whites and water until frothy. Add nuts; stir gently to coat. Combine sugar, pie spice and salt; add to nut mixture and stir gently to coat. Fold in raisins. Spread into two greased 15-in. x 10-in. x 1-in. baking pans.

Bake, uncovered, at 300° for 20-25 minutes or until lightly browned, stirring every 10 minutes. Cool completely. Store in an airtight container. **Yield:** about 10 cups.

Cheese Ball Snack Mix

(Pictured at right)

Mary Detweiler, West Farmington, Ohio

Folks really love the zippy burst of flavor in every bite of this fun snack mix.

    1-1/2 cups salted cashews
        1 cup crisp cheese ball snacks*
        1 cup Corn Chex cereal

        1 cup Rice Chex cereal
        1 cup miniature pretzels
        1 cup chow mein noodles
      1/2 cup butter, melted
        1 tablespoon soy sauce
        1 teaspoon Worcestershire sauce
      1/2 teaspoon seasoned salt
      1/4 teaspoon chili powder
      1/4 teaspoon hot pepper sauce

In a bowl, combine the cashews, cheese balls, cereals, pretzels and chow mein noodles. In another bowl, combine the remaining ingredients. Pour over cereal mixture and toss to coat. Transfer to an ungreased 15-in. x 10-in. x 1-in. baking pan. Bake at 250° for 1 hour, stirring every 15 minutes. Cool completely. Store in an airtight container. **Yield:** about 6 cups.

*Editor's Note: This recipe was tested with Planter's Cheeze Balls.

Slow Cooker Party Mix

Dana Hughes, Gresham, Oregon

This mildly seasoned snack mix is always a party favorite. Served warm from a slow cooker, the munchable mixture is very satisfying.

        4 cups Wheat Chex cereal
        4 cups Cheerios
        3 cups pretzel sticks
        1 can (12 ounces) salted peanuts
      1/4 cup butter, melted
        2 to 3 tablespoons grated Parmesan cheese
        1 teaspoon celery salt
      1/2 to 3/4 teaspoon seasoned salt

In a 5-qt. slow cooker, combine cereals, pretzels and peanuts. Combine butter, Parmesan cheese, celery salt and seasoned salt; drizzle over cereal mixture and mix well. Cover and cook on low for up to 3 hours, stirring every 30 minutes. Serve warm or at room temperature. **Yield:** about 3 quarts.

Microwave Snack Mix

Priscilla Weaver, Hagerstown, Maryland

I zap this fun snack in my microwave. The peanuts and pretzels come out so crisp and crunchy you'd think they were oven-baked.

- **1/2 cup butter**
- **2 teaspoons chili powder**
- **1 teaspoon ground cumin**
- **1/2 teaspoon garlic powder**
- **5 cups oyster crackers**
- **3 cups miniature pretzels**
- **2-1/2 cups salted peanuts**
- **2 tablespoons Parmesan cheese**

In a small microwave-safe bowl, combine butter, chili powder, cumin and garlic powder. Cover and microwave on high for 45-60 seconds or until butter is melted.

In a 3-qt. microwave-safe dish, combine crackers, pretzels and peanuts. Add butter mixture and mix lightly. Sprinkle with Parmesan cheese and toss to coat. Microwave, uncovered, on high for 7-8 minutes or until mixture begins to toast, carefully stirring every 2 minutes. Cool completely. Store in an airtight container. **Yield:** 10 cups.

Editor's Note: This recipe was tested in a 700-watt microwave.

Taco Tidbits

(Pictured above right)

Sharon Mensing, Greenfield, Iowa

This four-ingredient combination is a great change of pace from typical snack mixes. And it's a good thing the crispy treat is so simple to throw together. After one handful, your family will empty the bowl in no time.

- **6 tablespoons butter**
- **2 to 3 tablespoons taco seasoning**
- **8 cups Corn Chex cereal**
- **1/4 cup grated Parmesan cheese**

Place butter in an 11-in. x 7-in. x 2-in. microwave-safe dish. Cover and microwave on high for 60-70 seconds or until melted. Add taco seasoning. Stir in the cereal until evenly coated. Microwave on high for 1 minute; stir. Heat 1 to 1-1/2 minutes longer; stir. Sprinkle with Parmesan cheese; microwave for 1 minute. Stir; heat 1 minute longer. Cool. Store in an airtight container. **Yield:** 8 cups.

Editor's Note: This recipe was tested in an 850-watt microwave.

California Fried Walnuts

(Pictured at right)

Alcy Thorne, Los Molinos, California

Since we grow walnuts, they go into everything at our house. This recipe produces a scrumptious party snack.

- **6 cups water**
- **4 cups walnut halves**
- **1/2 cup sugar**

Oil for frying
1-1/4 teaspoons salt

In a large saucepan, bring water to a boil. Add walnuts; boil for 1 minute. Drain; rinse under hot water. In a large bowl, toss walnuts with sugar. In an electric skillet, heat 1/2 in. of oil to 350°. Fry walnuts for 5 minutes or until dark brown, stirring often. Drain in a colander over paper towels. Sprinkle with salt. Cool completely. Store in an airtight container. **Yield:** 4 cups.

MOCHA PUNCH

HOT CRANBERRY CITRUS DRINK

HOMEMADE EGGNOG

FANCY BERRY BEVERAGE

AUNT FRANCES' LEMONADE

MELON FRUIT SLUSH

BEVERAGES

Mocha Punch

(Pictured above)

Yvonne Hatfield, Norman, Oklahoma

I first tried this smooth, creamy punch at a friend's Christmas open house. It was so special and distinctive I didn't leave until I had the recipe. Having a frosty glass of this chocolate punch is almost like sipping a chocolate shake.

  1-1/2 quarts water
    1/2 cup instant chocolate drink mix
    1/2 cup sugar
    1/4 cup instant coffee granules
    1/2 gallon vanilla ice cream
    1/2 gallon chocolate ice cream
      1 cup heavy whipping cream, whipped
Chocolate curls, optional

In a large saucepan, bring water to a boil. Remove from the heat. Add drink mix, sugar and coffee; stir until dissolved. Cover and refrigerate for 4 hours or overnight.

About 30 minutes before serving, pour into a punch bowl. Add ice cream by scoopfuls; stir until partially melted. Garnish with dollops of whipped cream and chocolate curls if desired. **Yield:** 20-25 servings (about 5 quarts).

Slow Cooker Cider

Alpha Wilson, Roswell, New Mexico

I like to welcome family and friends into our home during the holidays with the wonderful aroma of this cider.

    2 cinnamon sticks (4 inches)
    1 teaspoon whole cloves
    1 teaspoon whole allspice
    2 quarts apple cider
  1/2 cup packed brown sugar
    1 orange, sliced

Place cinnamon, cloves and allspice in a double thickness of cheesecloth; bring up corners of cloth and tie with a string to form a bag. Place cider and brown sugar in a slow cooker; stir until sugar dissolves. Add spice bag. Place orange slices on top. Cover and cook on low for 2-5 hours or until cider reaches desired temperature. Remove spice bag before serving. **Yield:** 2 quarts.

Citrus Grove Punch

(Pictured below)

Susan West, North Grafton, Massachusetts

This pretty, sparkling punch brings in other members of the citrus family to blend with orange juice. Sparkling bubbles from the ginger ale give each sip a festive tingle.

    3 cups sugar
    2 cups water
    6 cups orange juice, chilled
    6 cups grapefruit juice, chilled
  1-1/2 cups lime juice, chilled
    1 liter ginger ale, chilled

In a saucepan, bring sugar and water to a boil; cook for 5 minutes. Cover and refrigerate until cool. Combine orange, grapefruit and lime juices and sugar mixture; mix well. Just before serving, stir in ginger ale. Serve over ice. **Yield:** 6 quarts.

Cranberry Apple Cider

(Pictured at right)
Jennifer Naboka, North Plainfield, New Jersey

I love to start this soothing cider in the slow cooker on nights before my husband goes hunting. Then he can fill his thermos and take it with him out into the cold. The cider has a terrific fruit flavor we both enjoy.

    4 cups water
    4 cups apple juice
    1 can (12 ounces) frozen apple juice concentrate,
      thawed
    1 medium apple, peeled and sliced
    1 cup fresh *or* frozen cranberries
    1 medium orange, peeled and sectioned
    1 cinnamon stick

In a slow cooker, combine all ingredients; mix well. Cover and cook on low for 2 hours or until cider reaches desired temperature. Discard cinnamon stick. If desired, remove fruit with a slotted spoon before serving. **Yield:** 10 servings (about 2-1/2 quarts).

Lemon-Lime Punch

Karen Engstrand, Alma, Wisconsin

This festive-looking green punch has starred at many holiday parties and other events. The recipe comes from a cookbook I won in a drawing when I was a child. The cover is lost now, and the pages are yellowing…but the recipes are as wonderful as ever.

    1 envelope (.13 ounce) unsweetened lemon-lime
      drink mix
    1 quart pineapple juice, chilled
    1 quart lime sherbet
    2 quarts ginger ale, chilled

Pour drink mix into a punch bowl. Stir in pineapple juice. Spoon sherbet into bowl; add ginger ale and stir gently. Serve immediately. **Yield:** about 3-1/2 quarts.

Dutch Hot Chocolate

Edna Hoffman, Hebron, Indiana

When my grandchildren come over to visit, they love to snack on homemade cookies along with mugs of my hot chocolate. Smooth and comforting, it has a light and sweet chocolate flavor with a hint of cinnamon. Dutch treats from my kitchen are a delectable part of our family's tradition.

    3 quarts milk
    6 cups water
 1-1/2 cups sugar, *divided*
    3 squares (1 ounce *each*) semisweet chocolate
    1 cinnamon stick, broken
  1/2 cup packed brown sugar

In a saucepan, combine the milk, water, 1 cup sugar, chocolate and cinnamon. Bring to a boil. Reduce heat to low; cook and stir until chocolate is melted. Add brown sugar and remaining sugar; cook and stir until heated through. Discard cinnamon stick. **Yield:** 18 servings.

Spiced Coffee

Joanne Holt, Bowling Green, Ohio

Even those who usually don't drink coffee will find this spiced blend with a hint of chocolate appealing. I keep a big batch simmering at a brunch or open house.

    8 cups brewed coffee
  1/3 cup sugar
  1/4 cup chocolate syrup
  1/2 teaspoon anise extract
    4 cinnamon sticks (3 inches), halved
 1-1/2 teaspoons whole cloves
Additional cinnamon sticks, optional

In a slow cooker, combine the first four ingredients; mix well. Place cinnamon sticks and cloves in a double thickness of cheesecloth; bring up corners of cloth and tie with string to form a bag. Add to slow cooker. Cover and cook on low for 2-3 hours. Discard spice bag. Ladle coffee into mugs; garnish each with a cinnamon stick if desired. **Yield:** 8 cups.

Wassail Punch

Dorothy Anderson, Ottawa, Kansas

The wonderful cinnamon, spice and fruit aroma of this punch fills the house.

    2 quarts apple cider
    2 cups orange juice
    2 cups pineapple juice
  1/2 cup lemon juice
  1/2 cup sugar
   12 whole cloves
    4 cinnamon sticks (3 to 4 inches)
Orange slices and additional cloves, optional

In a large kettle, bring the first seven ingredients to a boil. Reduce heat; simmer for 10-15 minutes. Remove cinnamon and cloves. Serve warm. If desired, stud orange slices with cloves and float in punch bowl. (Be sure bowl is safe for hot liquid.) **Yield:** about 3-1/2 quarts.

Homemade Eggnog

(Pictured above)

Pat Waymire, Yellow Springs, Ohio

After just one taste, folks will know this holiday treat is home-made, not a store-bought variety.

- 12 eggs
- 1-1/2 cups sugar
- 1/2 teaspoon salt
- 2 quarts milk, *divided*
- 2 tablespoons vanilla extract
- 1 teaspoon ground nutmeg
- 2 cups heavy whipping cream

Additional nutmeg, optional

In a heavy 4-qt. saucepan, whisk together eggs, sugar and salt. Gradually add 1 qt. of milk. Cook and stir over low heat until a thermometer reads 160°-170°, about 30-35 minutes. Pour into a large heatproof bowl; stir in vanilla, nutmeg and remaining milk. Place bowl in an ice-water bath, stirring frequently until mixture is cool. If mixture separates, process in a blender until smooth. Cover and refrigerate for at least 3 hours.

When ready to serve, beat the cream in a mixing bowl on high until soft peaks form; whisk gently into cooled milk mixture. Pour into a chilled 5-qt. punch bowl. Sprinkle with nutmeg if desired. **Yield:** 3-1/2 quarts.

Editor's Note: Eggnog may be stored, covered, in the refrigerator for several days. Whisk gently before serving.

Cherry Punch

Davlyn Jones, San Jose, California

Back in 1952, a co-worker gave me the recipe for this versatile, rosy punch. It's not too sweet, so it really refreshes.

My family and friends have sipped it at countless gatherings over the years—from picnics to the holidays.

- 1 can (6 ounces) frozen lemonade concentrate, thawed
- 1 can (6 ounces) frozen limeade concentrate, thawed
- 1 can (20 ounces) pineapple chunks, undrained
- 2 cups water
- 2 liters cherry soda, chilled
- 2 liters ginger ale, chilled

Lemon and lime slices, optional

In a blender, combine lemonade and limeade concentrates and pineapple; cover and blend until smooth. Pour into a gallon-size container; stir in water. Store in the refrigerator.

To serve, pour the mixture into a punch bowl; add cherry soda and ginger ale. Garnish with lemon and lime slices if desired. **Yield:** about 6 quarts.

Sparkling Grape Punch

Arlyn Kramer, Dumas, Arkansas

I rely on this lovely mauve-colored punch for quenching the thirst of my brunch guests. It's bubbly, fruity and simple to stir up for a crowd.

- 2 cups water
- 1 cup sugar
- 2 cups grape juice, chilled
- 1 cup orange juice, chilled
- 2 liters ginger ale, chilled

In a saucepan, combine water and sugar. Bring to a boil; boil for 3 minutes. Cool. Add juices and mix well. Stir in ginger ale just before serving. **Yield:** about 5-1/2 quarts.

Mock Champagne Punch

Betty Claycomb, Alverton, Pennsylvania

Of all the punch recipes I've tried, I keep coming back to this pretty, nonalcoholic one.

        1 quart white grape juice, chilled
        1 quart ginger ale, chilled
Strawberries *or* raspberries

Combine grape juice and ginger ale; pour into a punch bowl or glasses. Garnish with berries. **Yield:** 16 (1/2-cup) servings.

Hot Spiced Punch

(Pictured below)

Ruth Peterson, Jenison, Michigan

This punch is especially good when the weather is cold, and you need something to warm you up.

       12 cinnamon sticks (3 inches), broken
        4 teaspoons whole cloves
        2 teaspoons whole allspice
Peel of 1 lemon, cut into 1-inch strips
        9 cups white grape juice
        1 can (46 ounces) unsweetened pineapple juice
      3/4 cup lemonade concentrate
      1/2 cup sugar
Additional cinnamon sticks, optional

Place the cinnamon sticks, cloves, allspice and lemon peel in a double thickness of cheesecloth; bring up corners of cloth and tie with kitchen string to form a bag.

In a large kettle, combine the grape juice, pineapple juice, lemonade concentrate and sugar; add the spice bag. Bring to a boil. Reduce heat; simmer, uncovered, for 1 hour or until punch reaches desired temperature. Discard spice bag. Serve hot with additional cinnamon sticks if desired. **Yield:** 4 quarts.

Melon Fruit Slush

(Pictured above)

Jane Walker, Dewey, Arizona

I cut up fresh honeydew and cantaloupe for this slush, which I often serve as a dessert instead of ice cream. You can also vary the fruit depending on what's in season.

        1 can (20 ounces) crushed pineapple, undrained
        1 package (10 ounces) frozen sweetened sliced strawberries, thawed
        4 medium ripe bananas, cut into chunks
        1 cup cubed cantaloupe
        1 cup cubed honeydew
    2-1/2 cups water
      3/4 cup orange juice concentrate
      3/4 cup lemonade concentrate
        6 liters lemon-lime soda, chilled

In a blender, process the fruit in batches until smooth. Pour into a 3-qt. freezer container. Stir in the water and concentrates. Cover and freeze until icy. To serve, spoon 1/2 cup into a glass; add about 1 cup soda. **Yield:** 20-25 servings.

Punch Pointer

Chill all punch ingredients before mixing so that you don't have to dilute the punch with ice to get it cold. Or garnish a cold punch with an ice ring made from punch ingredients instead of water.

1/4 to 1/2 teaspoon ground ginger
1/4 teaspoon ground cinnamon
1/4 teaspoon ground nutmeg
4 fresh orange slices (1/4 inch thick), halved

Combine the first five ingredients in a slow cooker. Top with the orange slices. Cover and cook on low for 4-6 hours or until heated through. Stir before serving. **Yield:** about 1 quart.

Aunt Frances' Lemonade

(Pictured below)

Debbie Blackburn, Camp Hill, Pennsylvania

My sister and I spent a week each summer with Aunt Frances, who always had this thirst-quenching lemonade in a stoneware crock in the refrigerator. It tastes so much like fresh citrus. It made such a refreshing drink after a hot day running around the farm.

5 lemons
5 limes
5 oranges
3 quarts water
1-1/2 to 2 cups sugar

Squeeze the juice from four of the lemons, limes and oranges; pour juice into a gallon container. Thinly slice the remaining fruit and set aside for garnish. Add water and sugar to juices; mix well. Store in the refrigerator. Serve on ice with fruit slices. **Yield:** 12-16 servings (about 1 gallon).

Fancy Berry Beverage

(Pictured above)

Christine Wilson, Sellersville, Pennsylvania

We offer this fruity beverage to guests to add a festive touch to holiday gatherings. It pours up frothy, then separates into a dark pink base with a light foamy top. A slightly tart drink, it's wonderful with home-baked cookies.

2 quarts cranberry juice, chilled
1 quart vanilla ice cream, softened
1 package (10 ounces) frozen sweetened sliced strawberries, thawed and pureed
1-1/4 cups sugar
1 teaspoon vanilla extract
2 cups heavy whipping cream, whipped
1 quart ginger ale, chilled
Fresh strawberries, optional

In a large bowl or container, combine the first five ingredients; stir until smooth and the sugar is dissolved. Fold in whipped cream. Slowly add ginger ale; stir gently to mix. Pour into glasses. Garnish with strawberries if desired. Serve immediately. **Yield:** 5 quarts.

Peachy Spiced Cider

Rose Harman, Hays, Kansas

Welcome guests with the inviting aroma of this warm beverage. I served this spiced cider at a cookie exchange and received so many compliments. Everyone enjoys the subtle peach flavor.

4 cans (5-1/2 ounces *each*) peach *or* apricot nectar
2 cups apple juice

Banana Pineapple Slush

(Pictured at right)

Beth Myers, Lewisburg, West Virginia

This sunny tropical slush really refreshes on summer days and is perfect for brunches, showers, weddings and neighborhood parties.

✓ **Uses less fat, sugar or salt. Includes Nutritional Analysis and Diabetic Exchanges.**

- 4 cups sugar
- 2 cups water
- 1 can (46 ounces) pineapple juice
- 3 cups orange juice
- 3/4 cup lemon juice
- 1/2 cup orange juice concentrate
- 8 medium ripe bananas, mashed
- 2 bottles (2 liters *each*) cream soda
- 3 cans (12 ounces *each*) lemon-lime soda

In a saucepan, bring sugar and water to a boil over medium heat; cool. Pour into a freezer container; add pineapple, orange and lemon juices, orange juice concentrate and bananas. Cover and freeze. To serve, thaw mixture until slushy; stir in cream soda and lemon-lime soda. **Yield:** about 9-1/2 quarts.

Nutritional Analysis: One 3/4-cup serving (prepared with sugar-free soda) equals 119 calories, 0 fat (0 saturated fat), 0 cholesterol, 23 mg sodium, 30 g carbohydrate, 1 g fiber, 0 protein. **Diabetic Exchange:** 2 fruit.

Lemon Almond Tea

Brenda McCaleb, Nashville, Tennessee

Try this delightful dressed-up version when you want to serve something other than plain iced tea. I've used it for all sorts of events.

- 4 cups water
- 15 individual tea bags
- 3/4 cup sugar
- 3 quarts cold water
- 1 can (12 ounces) frozen lemonade concentrate
- 1 to 1-1/2 teaspoons almond extract

In a large saucepan, bring water to a boil. Remove from the heat; add tea bags. Cover and steep for 5-10 minutes. Discard tea bags. Stir sugar into tea until dissolved. Stir in cold water, lemonade concentrate and extract. Serve over ice. **Yield:** about 4 quarts.

Lemon-Berry Pitcher Punch

(Pictured on front cover)

Margaret O'Bryon, Bel Air, Maryland

If you need to satisfy a large group, you can double or triple the recipe for this refreshing beverage. The tangy combination of lemonade and cranberry juice is a real thirst-quencher on a summer day. But we like it so much, I serve it year-round.

- 1/2 cup sweetened lemonade drink mix
- 4 cups cold water
- 2/3 cup cranberry juice, chilled
- 1-1/2 cups lemon-lime soda, chilled

In a pitcher, combine drink mix, water and cranberry juice. Stir in soda. Serve immediately. **Yield:** about 6 cups.

Pineapple Strawberry Punch

Heather Dollins, Poplar Bluff, Missouri

We enjoyed this delicious drink at my wedding reception. Since then, it's been a must at Christmas gatherings and other special occasions. It's a fast and festively colored beverage.

✓ **Uses less fat, sugar or salt. Includes Nutritional Analysis and Diabetic Exchanges.**

- 2 packages (10 ounces *each*) frozen sweetened sliced strawberries, thawed
- 1 can (46 ounces) pineapple juice, chilled
- 4 cups lemon-lime soda, chilled

In a food processor or blender, puree the strawberries. Pour into a large punch bowl. Stir in the pineapple juice and soda. Serve immediately. **Yield:** 12 servings (3 quarts).

Nutritional Analysis: One 1-cup serving (prepared with sugar-free soda) equals 99 calories, trace fat (trace saturated fat), 0 cholesterol, 9 mg sodium, 25 g carbohydrate, 1 g fiber, 1 g protein. **Diabetic Exchange:** 1-1/2 fruit.

Tangy Fruit Punch

(Pictured above)

Ann Cousin, New Braunfels, Texas

A variety of fruity flavors mingles in this rosy refreshing punch. It's a popular beverage for a brunch, since its versatile sweet-tart taste goes wonderfully with all kinds of foods.

- 1 can (46 ounces) pineapple juice
- 1 can (12 ounces) frozen orange juice concentrate, thawed
- 3/4 cup lemonade concentrate
- 1 cup water, *divided*
- 1/2 cup sugar
- 2 large ripe bananas
- 1 package (20 ounces) frozen unsweetened whole strawberries, thawed
- 2 liters ginger ale, chilled

In a punch bowl or large container, combine pineapple juice, orange juice concentrate, lemonade concentrate, 1/2 cup water and sugar. Place bananas, strawberries and remaining water in a blender; cover and process until smooth. Stir into the juice mixture. Cover and refrigerate. Just before serving, stir in ginger ale. **Yield:** 25-30 servings (about 5 quarts).

Cranberry Party Punch

(Pictured below)

Cute cranberry-filled ice molds shaped like candy canes float in this refreshing five-ingredient fruit punch from the Taste of Home Test Kitchen. It's easy to stir up.

- 1 cup cranberries
- 1 cup crushed ice
- 4 cups cranberry juice, chilled
- 4 cups pineapple juice, chilled
- 1-1/2 cups sugar
- 1 tablespoon almond extract
- 2 liters ginger ale, chilled

Using three 4-in. candy cane molds or shape of your choice, arrange cranberries and crushed ice alternately in a striped pattern. Add cold water to fill molds. Freeze for 2 hours. To unmold, wrap a hot damp cloth around the bottom of the mold; invert onto a baking sheet.

In a punch bowl, combine the juices, sugar and extract; stir until sugar is dissolved. Add ginger ale. Place ice molds in bowl, rounded side up. Serve immediately. **Yield:** 4 quarts (20 servings).

Mock Eggnog

Susannah Wayman, South Jordan, Utah

I found a mock eggnog recipe in a newspaper, made a few changes and this is the result. We love it during the holidays.

- 2 quarts cold milk
- 1 package (3.4 ounces) instant French vanilla *or* vanilla pudding mix
- 1/4 cup sugar
- 1 teaspoon ground nutmeg
- 1 teaspoon vanilla extract
- 1/8 teaspoon salt, optional
- 1 cup heavy whipping cream
- Additional nutmeg, optional

In a mixing bowl, beat milk and pudding mix on low speed for 2 minutes. Beat in the sugar, nutmeg, vanilla and salt if desired. In another mixing bowl, beat cream until thickened, about 3 minutes. Stir into pudding mixture. Refrigerate until serving. Sprinkle with additional nutmeg if desired. **Yield:** about 2-1/2 quarts.

Raspberry Lemonade

Dorothy Jennings, Waterloo, Iowa

This crisp, tart beverage is a real thirst-quencher on a hot day. Pretty enough to serve at a bridal shower and refreshing enough to pour at a picnic, it's a fun change from iced tea or regular lemonade.

- 2 cans (12 ounces *each*) frozen lemonade concentrate, thawed
- 2 packages (10 ounces *each*) frozen sweetened raspberries, partially thawed
- 2 to 4 tablespoons sugar
- 2 liters club soda, chilled
- Ice cubes

In a blender, combine lemonade concentrate, raspberries and sugar. Cover and process until blended. Strain to remove seeds. In a 4-1/2-qt. container, combine raspberry mixture, club soda and ice cubes; mix well. Serve immediately. **Yield:** 3-1/2 quarts.

Icy Holiday Punch

Margaret Matson, Metamora, Illinois

It's easy and convenient to prepare the base of this slushy punch ahead. Its rosy color makes it so pretty for Christmas. I've also made it with apricot gelatin for a bridal shower. This fun beverage makes any occasion a bit more special.

- 1 package (6 ounces) cherry gelatin
- 3/4 cup sugar
- 2 cups boiling water
- 1 can (46 ounces) pineapple juice
- 6 cups cold water
- 2 liters ginger ale, chilled

In a 4-qt. freezer-proof container, dissolve gelatin and sugar in boiling water. Stir in pineapple juice and cold water. Cover and freeze overnight. Remove from the freezer 2 hours before serving. Place in a punch bowl; stir in ginger ale just before serving. **Yield:** 32-36 servings (5-3/4 quarts).

Hot Cranberry Citrus Drink

(Pictured above)

Shari Donaldson, Cummings, Kansas

This lovely rosy drink, with its appealing fresh fruit flavor, is not too sweet or too tart. I sometimes serve this hot beverage at Christmas or at brunch gatherings as an alternative to coffee, tea or cold juice.

- 1 package (12 ounces) fresh *or* frozen cranberries
- 2-1/2 quarts water
- 2 cups orange juice
- 1 cup sugar
- 1 cup pineapple juice
- 2 tablespoons lemon juice
- 3 cinnamon sticks (3 inches)

In a large saucepan, bring cranberries and water to a boil. Reduce heat; simmer for 5-7 minutes or until the berries pop. Stir in the remaining ingredients; return to a boil. Reduce heat; simmer, uncovered, for 25-30 minutes. Strain through cheesecloth; discard pulp and cinnamon sticks. Serve warm. **Yield:** 3 quarts.

Hot Beverages Hint

For hot beverages, avoid shattering the serving bowl by making sure the bowl is heat-resistant and by warming the bowl with warm water before adding the hot punch.

Summertime Strawberry Punch

(Pictured at right)

Mary McQueen, Woodstock, Ontario

This thirst-quenching drink is perfect for a summer picnic or family get-together.

  1 can (12 ounces) frozen pink lemonade
    concentrate, thawed, undiluted
  1 package (20 ounces) frozen unsweetened
    strawberries, partially thawed
1/4 cup sugar
  2 cups cold brewed strong tea
  2 liters ginger ale, chilled
Ice cubes

In a food processor or blender, combine lemonade concentrate, strawberries and sugar. Cover and process until smooth. Transfer to a large pitcher or punch bowl; stir in tea. Add the ginger ale and ice cubes. Serve immediately. **Yield:** 3-1/2 quarts.

Pennsylvania Milk Punch

Shirley Womer, Middleburg, Pennsylvania

Children of all ages will savor the nostalgic flavor of this refreshing punch. It reminds me of the orange creamsicles we enjoyed when we were young.

✓ **Uses less fat, sugar or salt. Includes Nutritional Analysis and Diabetic Exchanges.**

4 cups milk
1 quart orange sherbet, softened
1 pint vanilla ice cream, softened
1 liter lemon-lime soda

In a mixing bowl, beat milk, sherbet and ice cream until frothy. Pour into a punch bowl. Stir in soda. Serve immediately. **Yield:** 20 servings.
  Nutritional Analysis: One 3/4-cup serving (prepared with fat-free milk, fat-free ice cream and diet soda) equals 91 calories, 61 mg sodium, 3 mg cholesterol, 18 g carbohydrate, 3 g protein, 1 g fat, 0 fiber. **Diabetic Exchange:** 1 starch.

Rhubarb Slush Punch

(Pictured at left)

Diane Haug, Neenah, Wisconsin

For years, our family has toasted special occasions with this punch. It's easy to freeze, so we serve it year-round.

  6 cups chopped fresh *or* frozen rhubarb, thawed
  7 cups water, *divided*
  2 cups sugar
3/4 cup orange juice concentrate
3/4 cup lemonade concentrate
10 cups club soda, chilled

In a large saucepan, bring rhubarb and 4 cups water to a boil. Reduce heat; simmer, uncovered, for 5-8 minutes or until rhubarb is tender. Mash rhubarb; strain. Reserve juice and discard pulp. Add sugar, concentrates and remaining water to rhubarb juice. Transfer to a freezer container and freeze.
  Remove from the freezer 30-45 minutes before serving, scraping the surface as it thaws. Place equal amounts of slush mixture and club soda in each serving glass. Serve immediately. **Yield:** 10 servings.

Fruity Mint Punch

Linnea Rein, Topeka, Kansas

This sweet, refreshing drink has tea as its base. The mint is mild but lingers on the tongue. Fresh mint is simple to grow and so rewarding in recipes like this.

8 tea bags
1/2 to 3/4 cup chopped fresh mint
4 cups boiling water
1-1/2 cups sugar
6 ounces lemonade concentrate
6 ounces limeade concentrate
3/4 cup orange juice
3 quarts cold water

Place tea bags and mint in a heat-resistant pitcher or bowl; add boiling water. Let stand for 5 minutes; strain. Stir in sugar, lemonade and limeade concentrates and orange juice; refrigerate. Just before serving, place mint mixture in a large punch bowl; stir in cold water. **Yield:** 4-1/2 quarts.

Sherbet Punch

Jeanne Bunders, Wauzeka, Wisconsin

Lime is my favorite flavor for Christmas, but I make this same recipe with raspberry sherbet, too. Either way, this punch is wonderful to sip on.

1/2 gallon lime *or* raspberry sherbet, softened
1 liter ginger ale
2 cups lemon-lime soda
2 cups grapefruit *or* citrus soda

Just before serving, place sherbet in a punch bowl. Add ginger ale and soda; stir until sherbet is almost dissolved. **Yield:** 4-1/2 quarts.

Tropical Slush

Hollis Mattson, Brush Prairie, Washington

I first tried this refreshing beverage—with its tasty combination of citrus juices and mashed banana—at a church reception. It's perfect for serving at birthday parties, wedding showers, anniversary dinners and barbecues.

6 cups water, *divided*
5 medium ripe bananas
2 cups sugar
2 cans (12 ounces *each*) frozen orange juice concentrate, thawed
1 can (12 ounces) frozen lemonade concentrate, thawed
1 can (46 ounces) unsweetened pineapple juice
3 bottles (2 liters *each*) lemon-lime soda

In a blender container, process 1 cup of water, bananas and sugar until smooth. Pour into a large container; add the concentrates, pineapple juice and remaining water. Cover and freeze.

Remove from freezer 2 hours before serving. Just before serving, break up and mash mixture with a potato masher. Stir in soda. **Yield:** 40-50 servings (about 11 quarts).

Raspberry Iced Tea

(Pictured below)
Lois McGrady, Hillsville, Virginia

I treasure this recipe because of the make-ahead convenience it offers. A few common ingredients are all I need to serve this refreshing beverage.

4 quarts water
1-1/2 cups sugar
1 package (12 ounces) frozen unsweetened raspberries
10 individual tea bags
1/4 cup lemon juice

In a Dutch oven, bring water to a boil. Remove from the heat; stir in the sugar until dissolved. Add the raspberries, tea bags and lemon juice. Cover and steep for 3 minutes. Strain; discard berries and tea bags. Cool. Serve over ice. **Yield:** 16 servings (4 quarts).

General Recipe Index

This handy index lists each recipe by major ingredient. For specific types of appetizers, refer to the recipe list at the beginning of each chapter.

✓ *Recipe includes Nutritional Analysis and Diabetic Exchanges*

✓Recipe includes Nutritional Analysis and Diabetic Exchanges
Index

Alphabetical Index

This handy index lists every recipe in alphabetical order so you can easily find your favorite recipes.

✓Recipe includes Nutritional Analysis and Diabetic Exchanges

Index